Perfect CV

Max A. Eggert is Chief Psychologist with Transcareer, a consultancy that assists individuals in achieving their career dreams. Max first graduated in Theology before transferring to Psychology. He followed this with a Masters in Industrial Relations and postgraduate work in Clinical Hypnosis. When not writing, coaching or running seminars, Max has two other passions: riding his thoroughbreds and dancing Ceroc. As an Anglican priest he is an active member of the parish team at St Mary the Virgin in Waverley, Australia. Should you wish to be coached by Max, for him to provide a workshop, or speak at a conference then please email him at max@transcareer.com.au.

Other titles in the *Perfect* series

Perfect
CV

Max Eggert

BOOKS

Published by Random House Books in 2007

4 6 8 10 9 7 5 3

First published in the United Kingdom in 2005 by
Random House Business Books

Random House Books
Random House, 20 Vauxhall Bridge Road,
London SW1V 2SA

www.randomhouse.co.uk

Addresses for companies within The Random House Group Limited can be found at:
www.randomhouse.co.uk/offices.htm

The Random House Group Limited Reg. No. 954009

A CIP catalogue record for this book
is available from the British Library

ISBN 9781905211739

The Random House Group Limited makes every effort to ensure that the papers used
in its books are made from trees that have been legally sourced from well-managed
and credibly certified forests. Our paper procurement policy can be found at:
www.randomhouse.co.uk/paper.htm

Typeset in Sabon by SX Composing DTP, Rayleigh, Essex
Printed in the UK by CPI Bookmarque, Croydon CR0 4TD

For
Patricia Ann Benson

Contents

CHAPTER 1

PERFECT CV

A perfect CV is a CV that achieves the interview, no more, no less. When the CV puts your name on the interview shortlist, it has done its job.

WE START WITH A WORD OF WARNING

Without too much difficulty you can find lots of people only too willing to give you advice on how you should present your career in CV form. In fact, people who give advice on CVs are rather like economists – if you laid us end to end we might go to the moon and back and you would still be given different information. We differ because there are no rules about CVs, no absolutes, only principles and it is these principles which are the subject of this little book.

Some of the suggestions that follow you will love, others you will abhor. Please be selective because in the end you are going to be the person who will be batting off your CV. It has to be your document and consequently you must feel both comfortable and confident with it.

SOME GOOD NEWS

Very few people spend money on job search books so the fact that you have invested in this book will hold you in good stead. You have invested in professional advice so having read this book and cherry picked what you like, your CV will be far better than the sea of amateurs stuff that is out there.

MAKE IT SPECIAL

The life of corporate and graduate recruiters is dull enough already without everyone's CV being the same. Make your CV unique and special: take what follows as guidelines rather than ground rules, suggestions rather than shibboleths.

There is no bible or Ten Commandments on how to write CVs, but only ideas and concepts which have been proven in the job market by thousands of job hunters with whom I have been privileged to work.

You will receive as many different pieces of advice on your CV as the number of people to whom you show it. Before you take the advice ask yourself the Quality Control Question:

When did the person giving this advice last gain a job for themselves or for someone else on the basis of what they are telling me to do?

If their job success or experience is not recent, handle the information you are given with care.

Writing a CV is not difficult but it is onerous. If your CV is to be successful, it will take lots of time – first draft usually about six hours of creativity, determination and frustration. There are no short cuts to doing it properly.

You don't need luck in your job search, it just takes effort.

CHAPTER 2

The CV is the Ticket to the Job Race

The CV is not only the first thing the potential employer sees about you; more significantly it is the only part of the whole job selection process over which you as a job seeker have 100 per cent control. You can't control the availability of the sort of job you want, you can't control who gets shortlisted, you can't control the interview – although you might if you read another book from this series, *Perfect Interview*. No, you can only control how you look in your CV.

THE TICKET TO THE JOB RACE

Your CV won't win you the job because it is rare for anyone to get hired just on the strength of their CV alone, but your CV will get you the ticket to the job race. Your CV is the ticket to the candidacy, so it goes without saying that it should be letter perfect, neat, easy to read and well organized. Even if you achieved just that, your CV would be, in my experience, better than 60 per cent of those which are sent by job hunters today.

HOW THIS BOOK IS STRUCTURED

The Principles

We start with some obvious and some not so obvious principles. Interestingly enough most of them do not come from psychology but from sales. There is an obvious reason for this: in your CV you are selling a product, YOU. Think of yourself as a brand.

So many jobseekers, especially those who have been retrenched, fired or need an income stream quickly dash of a CV and then are surprised that it does not work. 'Fire, aim, ready' will not produce a good CV. It is a mistake to let your emotions get ahead of your intelligence when it comes to producing your own marketing brochure.

Some Do's

These are some of the basics of CV construction. However, remember the golden rule, if you don't think that this recommendation is for you, then don't use it. It is important that you feel comfortable with your final document.

Format and Structure

Now we can put some flesh on the skeleton. Again some of these are obvious but many make the mistake of laying out their CV in an application form format and, in most cases, this will not show you off to your best advantage.

Note again there are no rules and so take what you like. No one structure fits all circumstances and each of us has individual needs.

Don'ts

Not just the reverse of the do's because there are far more don'ts. All the don'ts have to be discovered by practice rather than by theory. Working with CVs and placing thousands of them every year into the job market, you soon learn what does not work. What has not worked is the main basis for the don'ts.

Again there may be special circumstances when it would be right for you to break the rule and do the don't. We even advise you when to do this.

Presentation

Obviously content is important, perhaps even the most important but if you do not present well then whatever you have to offer might not get the attention that it deserves.

Internet

Most large firms and recruiters use this medium. It is fast, effective and economical. It is also different so it is important that you incorporate the demands of cyber space into your job search.

Marketing

It is no good having a fantastic CV on your desk, it must find it's way to the job decision maker. So we give you some tips on marketing what to say and to whom to say it to.

Examples

Now here we are really going to confuse you – we not only show you what not to do but give you different examples of what to do. Confused? You will be because we don't want an interviewer saying 'So you read Max Eggert's book' because you have produced a standard one-off, one size fits all CV.

THE CV WRITER'S CREED

I promise that I will:

1. Be totally honest with myself and everything on my CV will be true. I will present myself in the best way that I can but I will not suggest that I am better than I am.
2. Be true to my values and not pursue positions which are in conflict with my beliefs.
3. Learn from my experience both my successes and my failures so that I maximize personal development opportunities.
4. Accept advice, reflect on it and incorporate it into my job search if I think it appropriate.
5. Be creative so that my CV is unique and represents not only my skills and experience but also me as an individual.
6. Be humble enough to change aspects of my CV that are not working for me. CVs are fashion items and I am prepared to go with the flow when it matches my aspirations.
7. Be thorough recognizing that there are no short cuts.
8. Be patient and not expect quick fixes recognizing that the better employer takes time and consideration in selecting the right candidate.
9. Take responsibility for my own job search and career because no one else can do it for me.
10. Always be the very best I can.

DO IT NOW

As you go through this book there are bound to be periods of intense frustration and pain as you write and

7

rewrite your CV. For the CV to capture the whole of your career and make you look attractive to a prospective employer in the first two or three pages is not going to be easy.

If you begin to get bored as you labour over your twelfth redraft just think how boring it is for someone to wade through yours and 200 others to get a short list of five.

Don't give up, keep going until you are pleased with the result. The worst case scenario is to see a job you want to go for and then only have an evening to produce your CV. So do it now as soon as possible.

As with footwear, so with your CV: Just do it.

Is your CV suffering from Resumania?
This is a deadly disease that strikes the job searcher and kills all hope of getting your CV short listed.

Symptoms are many and varied but the primary signs of this malady are:

- CV on brightly coloured paper and not A4 size
- CVs displaying strange fonts – gothic or Lucinda are classic symptoms
- CV with huge helpings of ego, verbage and puff
- CV with all that exciting additional irrelevant information such as ages of children, tax and passport numbers or spouse's occupation
- CVs with a sprinkling of spelling, syntax and grammatical errors
- CVs longer than four pages
- CVs giving salary details
- CVs with gaps in employment
- CVs with your photograph
- CVs attaching photocopies of your job description, references back to nineteen hundred and freezing together with certificates for life-saving
- CVs which are expensively bound

TEN GOOD REASONS FOR WRITING YOUR CV

When you write your CV it will:

1. Give you more focus upon what you are good at and consequently the best career options for you.
2. Help you to understand which of your many skills and competencies you wish to concentrate on and develop.
3. Act as your ticket to the job race.
4. Provide you with an opportunity to reflect on your achievements, thus enhancing your self-esteem and self-image.
5. Beat the competition on the first stage of your journey towards the rest of your career.
6. Encourage you to quantify your achievements and their benefits to your potential employer.
7. Be the best preparation for the interviews that are to come.
8. Help you identify gaps in your experience portfolio for your chosen career and what you should do about them.
9. Enable you to see your career in broad prospective.
10. Discover aspects about yourself you never realized before

Ten good reasons for doing it now.

CHAPTER 3

Looking To Turn You Down

Remember from the outset that at the CV stage of selection the recruiter is looking for reasons to turn you down and not to take you on! Advertisements these days are going to attract hundreds of applications, sometimes even thousands of replies is not that uncommon.

As a recruiter, if I have a pile of CVs, my main task is to reduce the mountain of 'job hopefuls' to a molehill of 'job possibles'. So that the maxim 'when in doubt, throw it out' is very much used by recruiters.

SEE ME, SEE ME!

The recruiter always thinks that he or she is good at their job simply because it never emerges how good the person, whose CV has just been rejected, might have been. Recruiters never gain any negative information about potentially brilliant candidates they have passed over at the sort stage. So right from the very start your CV has to be special, and state in as many ways as possible 'see me, see me.'

CHAPTER 4

No Gain Without Pain

'I got so fed up with writing my CV and then keeping it up to date' is a frequent cry of the job hunter. It is amazing that some people want to get a lifetime's career into a CV that takes less than one hour to write.

If you get bored with writing your CV just think how boring it is to read CVs day after day.

EIGHTEEN MILLION CVS

Here is a simple sum:

$$\frac{20\% \text{ of } 1.5 \text{ million} \times 5}{1,000 \times 2} \quad = \quad 750$$

Let me explain why you should have this number in mind when you are writing your CV. Say there were 1.5 million people unemployed and looking for work. Say that just one in five bother to write a CV. And supposing they send off just five CVs a week for 12 weeks, that is one per day for the average time it takes to gain a job. That is a staggering 18 million CVs in any one three-month period. If only half of those are sent to blue-chip firms in *The Times* Top 1000 firms, then that means that those firms are being sent something like 750 CVs a week. Now reading 750 CVs each week is what I call really boring. For your CV to have any chance of success, it has to be something very special.

Your CV has to be like a young plant in a tropical forest reaching up to the light. If it is to survive, it must use every trick and strategy that it can. In addition it must be realized that although there are no short cuts to the CV, the investment in time and effort will be well rewarded.

CHAPTER 5

How Many CVs?

In an ideal world there should be one CV specifically written and customized for each job, but today's job market requires you to send off hundreds of CVs to hundreds of potential employers because competition is fierce and quality opportunities are scarce.

Consequently, the CV has to be somewhat ubiquitous.

In my experience the serious job hunter needs 3 basic CVs, namely:

1. A CV built around your present job
2. A CV aimed at the next job in your career
3. A combination of 1) and 2) above

This should give you the basic requirement for most of your applications but remember there still will be a need to customize your CV, for instance: changing the ranking of your achievements around the required competencies. Or perhaps summarizing jobs that are not relevant to the position for which you are applying.

Advertisements for positions give away lots of information about the job on offer. So every time you apply for an advertised job your CV is going to be a cut and paste job for you to fit as closely as you can to the specification they are looking for.

KEEPING TRACK

Make sure you remember which CV you have sent to which employer. It sounds easy enough, but an amazing number of applicants forget. Some careful administration is needed here.

Don't scoff. We have had people turn up for the wrong job, on the wrong day, asking for the wrong interviewer and forgetting which CV they sent in for their application.

CHAPTER 6

The Words

Curriculum Vitae
From the Latin, which is 'The way your life has run'.

Résumé
From the French, meaning 'summary'.

For the job seeker a CV is a personal document outlining pertinent information needed by a prospective employer. It is to enable the employer to tell quickly whether or not a meeting would be worthwhile. If what is seen is liked, it will lead to an interview. If not, it won't and you and the selector will have both been saved the time and effort of an interview.

BASIC REQUIREMENTS

As with most of life, there are no absolutes and CVs are no exception. There are things which work in the job market and things which do not. What follows are some practical tips and ideas which have justified their inclusion throughout trial and error in the job market. The CV serves three basic requirements:

- To highlight your value to a potential employer
- To provide a structure and a curriculum for the interview
- To act as a record of the substance of the interview

Writing a CV is not difficult but if it is to achieve its purpose it will require time, effort, reflection, creativity and determination.

Above all, the CV must be written with the potential employer firmly in mind. Authors write with their readers in mind, advertisers with their potential customers in mind, and so must you. You are selling your skills and experience in the job market, and you must ensure that your personal brochure presents you in the best possible way to your potential buyer.

CHAPTER 7

Corect Speling

I bet the heading on this page jarred! It is obvious that everything in the CV has to be spelt correctly but you would be surprised how many have mistakes in them.

When you are only represented by two or three pages of A4 it takes just one small error for the selector to put you in the 'Polite Turn Down' pile.

WHAT SPELLING MISTAKES SAY ABOUT YOU

All sorts of things are incorrectly inferred from a spelling or typing mistake, including:

- You cannot spell
- You are lazy
- You are inattentive to detail
- You want to fail
- You could not represent the company
- You do not really want the job

There will be enough reasons for the recruiter to put you in the 'No' pile without you providing – by misspelling or the odd 'typo' – an additional reason.

It is not enough to run the CV through the spell check. This will catch the spelling errors but not the 'typos' and a typo will have the same effect on a selector as a spelling error.

SEW KNOW MOOR MISS CAKES!

CHAPTER 8

Use Short Sentences and Short Words

Your CV is going to be skimmed on the first pass and not read, so to make the document easy to work with by using short sentences. The sentence you have just read contains twenty-seven words. It is too long. Where you can, follow the style of the tabloids. Here sentences are about twelve words long. This style gives your CV a real punchiness. It becomes a dynamic document. Unless you are going for a job that requires style, keep your sentences short. English might be brutalized in the tabloids but the message gets across. So follow *The Sun* and look in *The Mirror* regularly.

In a CV complicated sentences are not helpful. Facts are more important than style. Say it quickly in the active tense.

Short words have the same effect. Words of more than three syllables are more difficult to understand at a glance. Those who have hundreds of CVs to work through have a hard enough job already. Be user friendly. Use short simple words.

CHAPTER 9

Positive and Minus

With a little bit of thought, it can be recognized that certain words are far more positive in their impact than others of roughly the same meaning.

For example:

> negotiated is stronger than liaised
> managed is more positive than supervised
> controlled is better than responsible for

Once the CV has been written every word needs to be examined carefully to see whether another more powerful or positive equivalent can be used.

A PASSIVE ATTITUDE

Generally speaking, the weaker words occur when the job holder is either passive or reactive to the work situation rather than in control of things.

Here are some more examples:

maintained	prevented	rejected
ordered	provided	revamped

| performed | recommended | specified |
| prepared | rectified | supported |

There is nothing intrinsically wrong with these words, but they give the impression of a passive person, someone who responds to situations rather than initiating them. With a little more thought and research more positive synonyms can be found and used to create a completely different impression – it is not what you do but the way you present it that achieves the interview.

CHAPTER 10

You Have the Right to Remain Silent

Remember, you do not have to tell the selector everything. One of the reasons that CVs fail is because they are far too long. Why is it that police forces around the world say 'You have the right to remain silent'? Because the more you say, the more you will entrap yourself. In CV terms the more you write, the more reasons you give the selector to turn you down.

So keep it brief. How brief is brief? – well, as a rule of thumb, if you say it all in two or three pages at the most there must be something wrong. There are many advisers who would say that just one page is all it takes. My view is that the more senior you are, the shorter your CV can be. Richard Whittington, for example, could get away with just the line 'Thrice Lord Mayor of London' and get a job as a City banker.

Our consultancy record to date is a 17-page CV which we had presented to us in Edinburgh. Not only was it 17 pages long, it was not until you waded through to page 16 that you discovered what it was exactly that the writer was currently doing.

So how long is long, our research at Transcareer suggests that three pages for a Senior Manager is more than enough and four pages for more junior positions. This myth might sound strange but the more senior you are, the more your current job says it all. In more junior positions, you want to show the spread of skills that you have. Please remember though, these are principles not rules. If you are a Senior Executive contemplating a career change away from your current position then you need to tell all to show how flexible you are.

THE 'MUST SEE' DECISION

The CV is a personal brochure and not your autobiography. How many product brochures tell you all the bad points as well as the good? Same with CVs; you need to give the selector only enough information to make the 'must see' decision. No more, no less.

There are no absolutes, but a reasonable rule of thumb is minimum of one page if you are a senior executive, two pages if not, and for everyone four pages maximum including a technical page if you are in engineering, computing or similar.

The CV is often used to provide a structure to the job interview. This purpose is frequently ignored or unappreciated by the job seeker. If you tell an employer you failed one of your A levels then the employer will talk about your failure. It is in your best interests to include only positive information and not feed the interviewer with negative points.

So you have a good deal of freedom to leave out information. What do you drop? Well, first of all, anything that is negative. Negative information is best explained at the interview when you have at least a fighting chance of explaining yourself.

If, for instance, you were fired five years ago because you disagreed with your boss but have had a fantastic career since, there is no rule that says you have to declare your dismissal on your CV. If you get asked at the interview why you left the firm five years previously you can then explain the circumstances.

THE 'GOLDEN DECADE'

Let me give an example. We live in a period which unfortunately and unwisely discriminates on age. Now if you think that your age is the most important thing which will commend you to an employer, then by all means put your date of birth immediately after your name and address.

This will go a little hard on you though if you live on the other side of what is called the 'golden decade' which is 30–40 for men, and because this world is sexist as well as ageist, 25–35 for women, then your chances of getting on the shortlist are somewhat slim.

If you must mention your age then put it on the back page. I would suggest you consider doing this anyway since there are few jobs in which how old you are is more significant than your academic qualifications or what you do. A word of caution – do not *omit* essential information such as age.

People in the computer industry have a good phrase, 'user friendly', and that is what your CV should be – user friendly, easy to work with. For example, if you have a higher qualification then please don't tell me that you first went to Monks Orchard Primary School and then on to Norbury Manor to get your GCSEs. Make yourself easy to work with by starting with your highest qualification first and going backwards. If you have a degree I know that you must have at least 5 GCSEs and 2 A' levels or the equivalent.

What often happens is that on leaving college many people prepare a CV for the first time. From then on, when the person wishes to change jobs their current employment information is tacked on to the college CV and it grows and grows like Topsy. Each time you make a trip into today's highly competitive job market, make a fresh start on your CV.

When I see a composite CV it first tells me that the writer is either lazy, can't be bothered or stupid. None of which I want in my firm. Just as I would not go to an interview wearing clothes that were fashionable a few years ago with a tie I had just bought nor would I do the equivalent with my CV.

THE REVERSE CHRONOLOGY RULE

Let us get back to being user friendly. Ask yourself the question:

'Which is more relevant to a prospective employer of my choice – what I did when I left school or what I am doing now?'

or

'Where are the skills and abilities I am currently selling – in my current job or in the one I took when I left school?'

The most recent experience is for most people the most relevant to their job hunt. So use this by employing the reverse chronological rule when writing about career and achievements.

There are exceptions to this. Supposing you started life as a teacher but for financial reasons switched to IT first as a programmer, then you became an analyst, then IT Manager and then you were made redundant or retrenched. On considering your options you would like to go back to teaching because the house is paid for and the children are off your hands. In this case you would lead with your teaching experience.

CHAPTER 11

Layout: Framed

Sometimes CVs give the impression that they have been shoe-horned on to the page. The content could be excellent but the visual presentation is awful. In the better restaurants food is arranged on the plate to look as good as it tastes. Food for interviewers ought to be arranged using the same principles – to make it look attractive.

If you look at a picture which has been framed, the margin at the bottom of the picture is usually larger than at the top or the sides. Look at the two diagrams below:

Figure 1

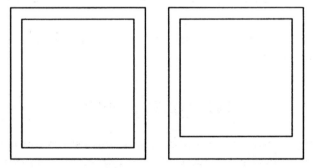

The one on the right is much more visually attractive. Lay out your CV in the same way.

GETTING THE RIGHT LAYOUT

Back pages of CVs are frequently only partially filled. This is a waste of opportunity to be able either to add relevant information or to spread your information so that it appears more attractive.

Half close your eyes and look at your CV – does the block of information look lopsided? Play about with the layout so that you gain a centrally balanced picture. See the diagrams below:

Figure 2

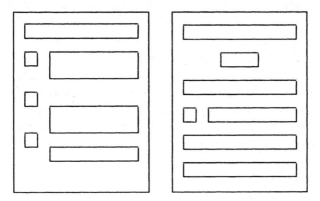

Again, it is the CV on the right which will create a better impression.

EVERYTHING COUNTS

Now, I know that it is nonsense to suggest that decisions by recruiters are made on visual impression and not on content. Of course, the content is by far the most important, but everything counts. If I have the job of sorting through six or seven hundred CVs and after I have been working for an hour or so I come across a messy CV which is poorly laid out, the temptation to move on to the next CV is often too great. Why should the selector spend time on your CV when the next one in the pile looks much more attractive?

Having worked hard on the content, make sure you present it in the most visually attractive way.

Please remember: If your CV looks like hard work it will be passed over.

You know this to be true. Every day you walk past shops with poor window displays and you don't even see them. Your CV is your career display – don't make the selector walk past it.

CHAPTER 12

To Justify, Or Not To Justify

Unless you want to show off your WP or DTP skills I would suggest that you do not right hand justify your CV. There are several reasons for this.

First, if your CV is right-hand justified like the pages in this book, it looks as if it is one of hundreds that you have produced. We know it is, but let the prospective employer think that your CV has been specially created and is a one-off for him or her.

AN OUTSIDER TRYING TO GET IN

Second, working documents in industry and commerce are not usually right-hand justified so when your CV arrives with its clean-cut right-hand margin, you are saying in a quiet way that you are an outsider trying to get in.

Finally, the ragged right-hand edge looks more visually interesting than the boxed edge made by a right justification.

The best thing to do is to make sure that the CV looks good. Try two versions, justified and unjustified, and go with the one that looks the better.

Exceptions again! If you indent for your achievements (and we will be covering this later) a right hand justification might make them stand out. This is a visual trick to make the eye of the selector fall to the achievement sections of your CV. Again play with different formatted versions and use the one which works best for you.

CHAPTER 13

Quality Paper

Would you turn up to the interview in your gardening clothes? Of course not, but it is surprising how many people submit CVs on cheap photocopying paper, usually 'borrowed' from their current employer.

Not that you are going to secure the interview on the basis of the quality of the CV paper, but image and first impressions are increasingly important these days.

PLAIN WHITE A4

Your CV should be on white standard A4 paper because that is what almost every organization uses today. For a PR or marketing job, perhaps a pastel or stronger colour could be used, but it is safer with plain white A4 of the best quality you can afford.

Do you really wish to have your personal brochure on cheap paper? No, you don't. Your CV paper should match your interview clothing in that it should be the best you can afford and that goes for the paper for the covering letters and the envelopes as well.

A word of warning: don't go overboard on this and get parchment or mottled paper. That is fantastic for posh party invitations but naf for CVs.

CHAPTER 14

Don't No. 1 – References

DON'T INCLUDE A REFERENCE

Job seekers often feel obliged to include references in their CV but it is obvious that any referee provided by the job hunter is bound to be friendly. Thus there is little advantage to the employer writing to a referee who has been nominated by the applicant. I have not come across an applicant yet who has invited a prospective employer to write to someone who will not provide a positive comment about the job seeker's work, attitude and disposition.

Employers are mainly interested in the relevance of your skills, experience and, more importantly, your attitudes, commitment and motivation. So while a member of the aristocracy may be impressive, or a local MP, police commissioner or other dignitary, they are not likely to be able to speak directly as to your suitability unless, of course, you want to go into politics or the police.

Consequently, if you feel bound to mention references then the simple statement, 'References available on request' should suffice.

MINIMAL INFORMATION

Following a decision in the House of Lords against an employer who gave a true, but damaging, reference to another employer about a potential employee, most employers, or their HR departments, will only give minimal information. Employers are usually more interested in qualitative data than quantitative. How hard you worked, or what aspect of your work you found interesting or did well is far more telling than bald statements of your job title and how long you spent in that job.

For these reasons, most references are taken up over the telephone and given off the record. In spite of the fact that most large firms have policies about not providing references except through the HR department these rules are not always kept.

What would one of your previous bosses say about you if he or she was asked:

- What did he actually do?
- How well did he do it?
- What was her major contribution to the department?
- How did she get on with other people?
- Was he a self starter?
- Could she be left unsupervised?

Obviously the truth will out but you can certainly help the truth along in a variety of ways.

YOUR IDEAL REFERENCE

After you have completed your CV a useful discipline is to write out an ideal reference for yourself. What would you like your previous boss to say about you? How could you justify all the points you wanted made about your work and your approach to it? Once you have done this, I would suggest you telephone your potential referees and bring them up to date with your career aspirations, plans and actions. (This is not always appropriate with present employers except in some public sector jobs where you are expected to move on regularly.) Having told your referees about your plans you can then refresh their memory about your recollections of your performance, with statements like 'You remember when I did 'x', you said it was good because . . .' will at least help them recall your good points. After you have spoken to them ensure that they have a copy of your CV as a reminder of all your achievements.

Particularly important when you want to change your career is to emphasize those aspects of your job and skills profile which are allied to your new sphere of aspirations.

The Reference Rule
So the basic rule is give your referees' names as late as possible in the selection process. If you hold back till after the interview(s) then so much the better because by then not only will you have given a lot of information but you also will have gained a great deal of intelligence about the job. Armed with these insights as to what they really want in a candidate, you will then be able to first think about who would be the most suitable referee to speak for you and secondly to brief them giving them all the information that you have about the job and their ideal candidate.

This is far more effective. Which of the following would impress you most if you were a Sales Manager recruiting staff.

Referee 1
John is excellent, always hardworking and gives 100%. Very pleasant is his manner and gets on well with everyone.

Or

Referee 2
John is a very hard working salesman who gets on well with everyone. He has the knack of generating new sales because he always gives 100%, he is tenacious right up until he closes the sale. His after-sales service is also faultless.

CHAPTER 15

Don't No. 2 – Photographs

What you must remember here is that for most of our history as humans we have been swinging around in trees, painting wode on ourselves and eating each other. Our primal instincts have taught us to look at another person and very quickly form an opinion about that person. We think yes – no, good – bad, like – dislike. In certain states of the US, employers are legally forbidden to ask candidates to send a photograph, simply because opinions form very quickly on visual information alone. So unless you were blessed by birth by being in the top five per cent for traditional good looks and are photogenic, you're likely to fall victim to visual discrimination. If the research finds that traditionally good-looking criminals get shorter sentences than ordinary-looking criminals, then what chance have you got as an applicant if, like the rest of us, you are just average in the looks department?

The media is an industry committed to stereotype and image making. Every newscaster is both handsome and authoritative. Someone could be an eight stone weakling and still be able to read the news, but I've not seen one yet. If you are just ordinary to look at, and most of us are, do not include a photograph.

A PROFESSIONAL, NOT A BOOTH

If a photograph is called for then invest money on this aspect of the job search project. The photographic booths in railway stations do a great job in producing snaps for passports and travel cards but they are not good enough for CVs. Go to a professional portrait photographer and tell him or her exactly what you want. Take along pictures from business journals or company corporate literature that you like and brief the photographer on the image you wish to project. Sometimes it is helpful to decide on three adjectives to describe the image you feel you have or you wish to project and tell the photographer that you want to look:

competent, dynamic and hardworking
or
professional, thorough and reliable
or
creative, enthusiastic, dynamic

Whatever three words suit you, and are appropriate to the type of job you are pursuing, ask to be photographed in a half smile. People looking at photographs of individuals with a half smile rate them as more intelligent, more friendly and with better interpersonal skills. The sort of things you would want in an employee anyway.

HERE WE HAVE TO BE SEXIST

If you are male and normally wear glasses, keep them on for the photograph. Again research suggests that males wearing glasses are rated as more intelligent, so do a Clark Kent rather than a Superman.

A word of warning here, not only for the photograph but also for the interview, make sure your glasses are in an appropriate style. Eyewear these days is fashion-wear and some males, presumably because glasses don't wear out by looking through them, wear glasses that came out of the ark. It makes you look old and the job market is ageist.

The job market is also sexist, even with female recruiters, so here is the advice for women. It is an unfair world and the same research quoted above suggests that wearing glasses makes females look frumpy or disorganized. Yes it is still sexist out there in recruitment land so you have to be like Wonderwoman and remove your specs when going into the selection game. Keeping your hair in a French Roll is OK though!

However, the basic rule still is: don't include a photograph unless you have to and if you must send a photograph spend money on getting it right.

WEAR DARK CLOTHES

Apparently dark clothes make you look more powerful so providing they suit you, this is the style for the interview. Be careful with 'dress down' firms though, so do some checking first. Even so dark slacks and dark button down shirts have the same effect.

Photographers are experts at making you look attractive but for females don't allow them to make you look sexy unless of course looking sexy is part of the job.

WARNING

With the advent of IT companies starting in garages and more interest in the product and the technology than in the image, we have seen a gradual erosion of formal work wear – suit, collar, tie. Make sure before you send your photograph that you emulate the dress code of the organization.

And finally a tip for men. Facial hair is out. Only six per cent of men have beards in the western world and most of them work in teaching, IT research or are psychologists where beards are almost part of the uniform. Rather than fall victim of a stereotype (men with beards are lazy, have something to hide, have weak chins etc) be clean shaven until you get the job. Additionally, if you are forty plus and graying then facial hair makes you look much older. Delivering toys at Christmas is the only job we know where a grey beard is useful. We don't know what the salary is but we do know it's a one-day-a-year job.

CHAPTER 16

Don't No. 3 – Salary

The iron rule of wages says that employers will pay you as little as they can to get you, motivate you and prevent you from leaving. Salary, then, is a negotiation point and to get this in perspective we must take a small excursion into the rules of negotiation (because I presume you wish to gain as much as salary as you can for your services).

The second rule of negotiation is 'only negotiate from power' (the first being only negotiate with decision-makers). When you are one of 150 or so other candidates who respond to a job advert, you have no power. So then is not the time to mention salary or what you want.

When you get on the shortlist you are one of perhaps five people but this is still not the time to mention pay and conditions.

Now, supposing you are the last candidate in the ring, do you have power? You bet. If the prospective employer turns you down now he or she knows that the whole recruitment process is going to start all over again and that is worth real money to you.

AS LATE AS POSSIBLE

Always, always, always leave salary negotiation as late as possible in the selection process. The little 'c' before the salary section in an advert for a job stands for 'circa' and in salary terms that can mean as much as ten per cent above or ten per cent below. Remember – if you start on a low salary with a firm you will stay low. One of the reasons for changing jobs is to improve your financial situation so employers expect you to negotiate. This point is covered in great detail in the book *Perfect Interview*, but for the time being don't include a figure for expected salary on your CV.

You may be writing to one of those firms that gives a low basic wage but lots of benefits – like a super fully serviced car, mortgage subsidy, your telephone bill paid and holidays which can be linked to business trips to the company's offices in the West Indies, Miami or Hong Kong. They are offering a basic £40,000 plus all these add-ons. They see from your CV that you are earning £43,000 without all the benefits but do not shortlist you because you are earning too much! So please, don't include salary. If you insist on putting something then I would suggest the phrase 'Salary is negotiable at interview'.

WHAT THE PROFESSIONALS REQUIRE

Sending your CV to agencies and headhunters, however, is different. These firms are paid a commission (sometimes as high as 35 per cent) of first year's earnings. They have a vested interest in getting as much for your 'head' as possible. In the salary stakes they are going to be on your side, so provide them with details of current package and, of course, what you would like to earn. You will get the benefit of some realistic feedback on your market worth.

Letting agencies know how much you earn and how much you expect (or will move for) does not preclude salary negotiations with your employer.

CHAPTER 17

Be Unique

If the employer writes the advert well and specifies exactly what is required then about 80 per cent of the CVs that are received will be from people like yourself who actually fit the specification. You will have had the same qualifications, the same sort of experience, so how can you appear different in a positive way? I would suggest from your achievements in a non-work situation – particularly if you have held an office or a position to which you were elected. For example:

Elected Treasurer of the College Geological Society
Elected Secretary of the PTA
Elected to the Committee of xyz

What does this term 'elected' mean? It says in a very quiet way – 'Look, my peers and colleagues outside the work context think that I am reliable, honest, responsible and trustworthy enough to be elected and to serve them in this or that capacity.'

Similarly words like 'nominated', 'selected', 'chosen' and 'invited' create the same dynamic image.

SPORTING ACHIEVEMENTS

Now, not all of us hold public offices or are members of the Rotary Club, the Lions or Mothers Union – although, if you are, they are worth mentioning. What about sporting achievements current or past? Even if you are past 50 years you can always tuck in somewhere that you represented your house, school or team at some particular sport.

I have worked on the CV of a Scotsman and a South African. The first acted as coach for the volleyball national team and the second was captain of a national youth team. Neither had his considerable sporting achievement on his CV.

What about your interests? You could put 'reading', but how much more interesting if you put:

The English Novel prior to 1930

or

Modern autobiographies post 1952.

THE FOOTBALL CLUB ADMINISTRATOR

I recently met a lady who had a very modest job in a lighting factory in Wiltshire. Twenty years previously, because her son was fanatical about football and had no one to play with, she organized first a football team, then a league and is now administrator of the town's local football club which is affiliated to the Football Association. Now, if I were an employer looking for good administration skills, interpersonal skills and determination, her achievements outside work would say it all.

CHAPTER 18

More Interest in Interests

Just two more things on outside interests and activities. (Not too many, otherwise the employer might think that you will not have time for work.) What you spend your disposable income on or your free time on tells a potential employer a great deal about you, your values, your motivation and, in some cases, your intelligence.

For instance, suppose someone had as her interests:

- Bridge at county level
- Crosswords
- Software design

she is likely to be:

- Intellectually able
- Good at problem solving
- Precise and possibly competitive

Suppose someone had:

- Squash
- Entertaining
- Restoring classic cars

he is likely to be:

- Competitive
- Sociable
- Possibly practical

LET COLLEAGUES HAVE A SAY

What interests will you declare on your CV? Ask some friends at work – who do not know you socially – 'What image does this create for you of someone?' and then give them your three interests. Is what they say the image you want to present?

Don't forget, the primacy rule works here as well. Here is an example:

- Translating medieval German mystery plays into English
- Television – especially drama
- Family – enjoying my young children

gives a completely different picture to the following:

- Family
- Television
- German translations

Notice here I have changed the order of the interests. This is because an employer could probably use German and so it takes advantage of the primary effect.

The last point on interests really applies to the whole CV. Remember interviewers eat what you feed them. If it is in your CV then be prepared not just to be asked questions about what you have written but to be tested to destruction.

If you are really stuck for an impressive interest then

put 'Current Affairs' and make sure you read the last three editions of *The Economist* and *Time* before you go for the interview.

If you are going to be interviewed by a senior board member, look them up in *Who's Who* and see what their interests are.

For obvious reasons leave out those interests you have which may cause an eyebrow to raise. Personally alarm bells go off for me when I read about people jumping out of perfectly good aircraft, hang off tall buildings on the thinnest of ropes or jumping from tall scaffolding with their feet tied to elasticated rope. Unless you are going for a job with an extreme employer the advice is go easy on the extreme interests.

BE PREPARED – TO EXPAND

Woe betide you if you can't expand in detail on what you put down. Frequently, when I was a full-time recruiter, I would see that someone had put reading as an interest and then at interview was unable to tell me quickly what was the last book they read. I once asked a young man at Sussex University to tell me about his interest in films, only to be told that he had seen a certain Clint Eastwood film all of three times. If you fail the credibility test in one part of your CV, it contaminates the whole CV. Just like those people at interview who use the phrase, 'Well, to be really honest . . .' and make you wonder about the veracity of the whole interview. Be prepared to talk fluently in the interview about your interests.

It is often possible to talk about your interests and weave in skills and competencies required in the job you are going for. So in preparing your CV think which of your interests could help you in this way.

CHAPTER 19

The Whole Truth

As I've said before, interviewers eat what you feed them and as most interviewers are not trained in this basic management skill, you can expect your CV to form the basic structure of the interview. It is absolutely paramount that everything on your CV can be verified and is true. If you cannot justify or speak to any part of your CV, your entire credibility will be lost and your chances of a job offer will be minimal.

NO FICTION, PLEASE

Omissions are permissible. That is to say, you can leave out negative information but be prepared to be challenged on the 'gaps' during the interview.

Just as you would not wish to join an employer who lied about your salary or career prospects, by the same token you should not invent qualifications you do not have or fictitious employment. These things are easily checked and, even if you are taken on, could be used as grounds for dismissal.

So the vote is 'Nothing but the truth'. BUT with the corollary 'Not the whole truth' because you don't have to include negative information. Why damage your chances?

In selection as in life: 'What might damage you is yours to know theirs to find out'. Is this unfair? Perhaps so but I have never seen a job advert that says, 'We laid off 33% of our indirect staff last year and hopefully now we have our financial situation sorted we are now looking for . . .' And in this case it is 'Theirs to know and yours to find out.'

CHAPTER 20

Use the Back Page and Put it on the Right

If you must say something which is not in your favour, then here are two tips. First put the bad news on the back page; and second, put it on the right-hand side.

PUTTING IT IN PERSPECTIVE

Put it on the back page so that at least the selector will read all the good stuff first, and any potentially negative information can be put into its appropriate perspective. For example, if the positions which you are applying for usually require someone of graduate status, and you have no degree but you have the appropriate experience, then structure your CV so that your career outline and details appears before the section on your education.

In fact if you do not have a degree and you are likely to be in competition with all those clever clogs with the letters after their name then leave out your whole education section. Chances are it will not be 'seen' on the CV cull.

Now let me explain why the right-hand side of your CV should be used. CVs are usually skimmed not read. They are gone through very quickly to gain a shortlist pile and a somewhat larger PTD (Polite Turn Down) file. When people skim for information, because they read from left to right, the left-hand side of the CV is read with far more attention and accuracy than information appearing on the right-hand side.

CHAPTER 21

Career Summary

Constructing the career summary is perhaps the most important and significant preparation for the CV. Whether or not you decide to use a career summary in your final CV, it is still a very useful discipline.

A career summary is a simple statement of thirty or so words that encapsulates your career aspirations and what you wish to sell in the market place. Imagine that you only have thirty or so words to convince a prospective employer to hire you. This process will concentrate the mind and focus the reader on what exactly it is you wish your CV to project.

The summary brings three potential benefits:

- First, it will help you become quite clear on which of your skills you wish to utilize and the shape of the career or job you want.
- Second, when placed strategically after your name, address and telephone number, it will act like a banner headline for your CV. In jargon terms, it acts as a pre-conditioning statement, that is, it conditions the reader to anticipate positive information about you.
- Third, a career statement can be used rather like a go/no-go gauge in quality control. Everything that

you wish to put on your CV should in some way support and justify the career statement. If you wish to include something about yourself which does not match the criteria of your career summary, then it may be wise to censor the item.

Developing a thirty-word career statement starting with a blank page can be quite a difficult exercise so you might like to try the following approach using a 'mind map' and the 'mnemonic' for the SAKE of your career.

SAKE

SAKE stands for the four different areas of yourself in which a prospective employer has an interest, namely your:

- Skills
- Attitudes
- Knowledge
- Experience

So here is the procedure:

1. Take a sheet of A4 paper – it works even better on A3 because you have more room – and put your name in a circle in the centre and then from the circle four arms coming off with Skills, Attitudes, Knowledge and Experience (see figure 3).
2. Now, just think about yourself in these areas, in terms of what you have, what you have done and what you have to offer a future employer. Let your imagination ebb and flow, jotting down anything and everything that comes to mind.

You can show your mind map to your partner, to a good friend or a business colleague whose views you value, because we sometimes miss the obvious or even devalue what we have to offer.

3. Next, go through your mind map, first taking out all the things you don't want to do, or use. Having done this, then rank in order all those aspects about yourself a potential employer would be interested in. This will give you the curriculum for your career summary.
4. Write your career summary in the third person singular as if you were an employment agency sending out details about yourself to a potential employer (See page 58 and Chapter 49).
5. Continually revise your career statement until you feel comfortable with it.

Figure 3 Personal Career Statement

Develop a mind map for your career to date, using the structure below:

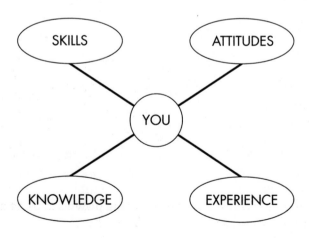

On this page you will see an example of how this structure has been used by a computing specialist.

Figure 4 Personal Statement Mind Map

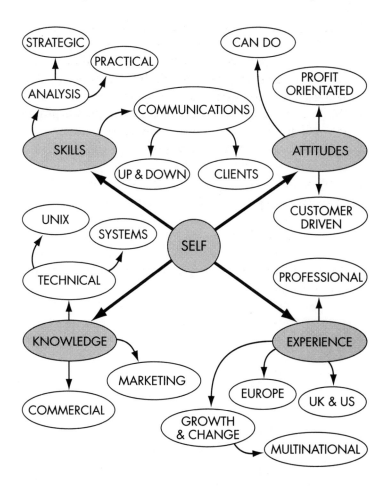

By playing with these concepts this individual was able to develop the career statement overleaf.

CAREER SUMMARY

A senior marketing professional with significant management experience gained with major US and European high technology multinationals.

An effective thinker and doer offering proven strategic planning, business management and communication skills. Able to work effectively at all levels in organizations with the ability to manage change and achieve commercial profit targets.

Further examples of career statements can be found in Chapter 49.

A good test of a CV is to give it to a friend for sixty seconds and then take it back from them and ask them to briefly summarize you as an applicant. If your CV has done what it is supposed to do then your friend should come up with something like your career statement.

Career Statements are still popular with small employers but the larger employers and recruiters recognise them as 'puff statements'. Today much more popular are skills or competency profiles.

However, this still does not detract from the value of the Career Statement as a preparation activity because:

- It helps you edit your CV. Everything the CV contains should support the career statement if it does not then cut it out.
- It helps you think through precisely what you are offering to the job market.
- It will help you answer the third question of the interview –

'Tell me about yourself'

(*The first two questions are usually rapport questions to settle you down such as 'How did you get here?' and an irrelevant question such as 'Is it still raining?' or 'Did you watch the game last night?' For more information please see one of my other books in this series *Perfect Interview*.)

• It helps with the ego especially if you are out of work or have been made redundant.

Instead of telling yourself 'I am redundant' which you need like a hole in the head, you can say:

'I am a qualified chicken sexer with a vast experience of breeding in all types of table foul specializing in . . .'

I am sure you get the picture.

CHAPTER 22

First Things First – Again

If you were a prospective employer what would be significant if you were looking for an employee? Put these facts in order of importance:

- Who you worked for
- When you worked for them
- What you actually did

I'm sure you came up with the right answer, which is:

- What you did
- Who you did it with
- When you did it

And yet we rarely see the individual's career history set out in this way in CVs.

SETTING IT OUT

It makes sense to put on the left-hand side what you did – recalling what I said about reading from left to right, put the important things on the left. In the centre of the page goes the organization that you work for – you don't need the address at this stage, it takes up too much room – and the dates go on the right-hand side. If you have had lots of jobs and you are worried about seeming to be a job hopper, or if you are a woman returner who has had a career break, you are more likely to create a favourable impression this way.

CAREER TITLES

You remember what I said about the eye skimming? Well, not only does it skim from left to right, but also from top to bottom. If on the left-hand side you just have a list of dates this does not convey very much information, but if I can see a list of career titles this creates an impression. In the following two examples, for instance, if I just skip down the left-hand side of the page and see:

1. Regional Sales Director
   Sales Manager
   Sales Rep
   Sales Administrator

2. D.P. Manager
   Operations Manager
   Senior Analyst
   Analyst/Programmer
   Programmer

At a glance a whole career unfolds, presenting the impression of a career which is still advancing and not of someone who only stays in a job a short while before moving on.

Whilst we are talking job titles if you have a title which would only mean something to someone in your organization then do a translation for your CV readers. If a reference is likely, be sure and check with your previous employer that this is okay to do so.

Sometimes quite humble job titles camouflage very senior positions. Recently I was working with someone from the defence industry whose job title was Team Leader: Project York refit. He had a colossal job managing a £112 million budget. With his employer's blessing we rechristened him to be Operational Projects Director. Re-labelling the job cost the old employer nothing but increased the 'CV see me factor' tenfold.

Mind you, you have to be careful. We were working with a production manager for a small company in Australia who wanted his title changed to Executive Production Vice President Southern Hemisphere. Oh really!

CHAPTER 23

Achievements, Not Just Responsibilities

People are sometimes too lazy to write their own CVs, and just crib one from their job descriptions by writing down all their responsibilities. I suppose that is better than nothing, but anybody can be given responsibilities. It does not really say what you did or did not do. You should also remember that when HR departments write job descriptions they are doing so for use in pay grading and appraisal assessment, not so that an individual can get a job elsewhere. Who in their right mind would want a CV that includes information written by someone else? It is rather like trying to sell a product using the raw material procurement specification and not developing any sales literature.

It would be wise to remember that employers write job descriptions so that they can hire, appraise and fire you. They don't construct them with the thought in their mind 'how can I help this person get a job?' So do not include job descriptions. Another reason is that the content of the description will be so specific to your old job it will knock you out of the box for the one you are going for which is bound to be different in a number of ways.

When you write about your job don't say what

someone else asked you to do based upon your job description but say what you actually did and how good you were at it.

THE ACHIEVEMENT PRINCIPLE

This we call the achievement principle. A storeman may be responsible only for stock, but a reduction in slow moving stock of 17 per cent and inventory levels reduced by 50 per cent are achievements.

Taking charge of sales in Surrey and Kent is a responsibility; continually selling over target by not less than 15 per cent in any one period is an achievement.

Basically, what you are claiming by highlighting an achievement is 'Look, I did this for them, I can do it again for you.' Lord Byron said something along the lines of 'If you want to know what a man will do in the future, look to his past'. In psychology we say the best predictor of future performance is past performance. So what we are saying here is – make your CV achievement rich.

CHAPTER 24

Achievements are FAB

There is a very simple process for getting your achievements down. It is called FAB (and comes from sales) – F stands for 'Feature'; A for 'Analysis'; and B for 'Benefit'.

F FOR 'FEATURE'

First of all, list all the things that you have actually done in a job. All those special successes, the times when you thought to yourself, 'I really did well there' or 'I really earned my salary there'. These are the highlights of your job. These are all the 'F's for Feature.

ADD IN THE NUMBERS

Now, we must work on the A. A is for 'Analysis'. We must analyze the feature. What was it, how big was it, who was involved, what were the savings to the company? Ask yourself the question, 'Is there any way I can get a number attached to the feature – a quantity, a percentage, anything that can be measured?' Reasons for this are both simple and obvious. If an achievement has a number attached to it, it looks more impressive, more credible and more under-standable. For instance, we could take the achievement:

Supervised the research of microbiologists

Let's work with that. How many microbiologists, what grade were they, what type of research, how did you supervise them? Working through these types of questions we get to this achievement:

Supervised a multi-disciplinary team of eight gradu-ate microbiologists, directing research into enzyme technology.

Help the gatekeepers to say 'yes'
As an HR manager in charge of recruitment, I might not know much about microbiology or enzyme technology, but I do understand the words multi-disciplinary and directing and the number eight. So not only does it sound more impressive, you help those people we call 'gatekeepers' to say 'yes'. Gatekeepers are people like those in human resources who control the gate through which candidates pass into the firm. They don't have the final say in who gets taken on but they do have a power to say who gets seen.

So a quick recap: which sounds better to you?

Supervised the research of microbiologists

or

Supervised a multi-disciplinary team of eight gradu-ate microbiologists directing research into enzyme technology.

I know which I would prefer.

SELLING THE SIZZLE

Let's now deal with the B. This comes straight from an established sales technique which suggests that people don't buy features, but do buy benefits.

For instance, I don't buy my car because it is a Turbo version, has a sun roof and central locking, I buy it because:

> I can accelerate quickly, have fresh air in the car on a hot day and when I park I can secure the car easily.

In other words, I want the benefits brought by the features, not the features themselves – so sell the sizzle not the sausage.

SO – WHAT?

It does not always work, but in the achievements section you should try to get in as many benefits to the company as possible. Use a very simple mechanism to do this. Ask yourself the question 'So what?' – 'So what was the company able to do that it could not do before?' 'So what was the advantage gained by the company as a result of this achievement?' Perhaps an example will help me explain. The basic achievement is:

> Raised venture capital.

Add the 'A' for Analysis:

> Raised £5m venture capital from Holland and the City.

Add 'B' for Benefit:

> Raised £5m venture capital from Holland and the City, enabling the company to grow without the requirement to consolidate the European expenses on the US balance sheet.

The HR Manager doing the initial selection might not know too much about balance sheet consolidations, but it sounds good, doesn't it?

AN ENGINEERING EXAMPLE

Let's take an engineering example:

Here is the 'F' for Feature:

> Analyzed video systems for marketing.

Here is the 'A' for Analysis:

> Analyzed advanced video systems for computer orientated go/no-go decision for marketing.

Here is the 'B' for Benefit:

> Analyzed advanced video systems for computer orientated go/no-go decision for marketing, thereby giving technical approval for the company's most profitable product.

Listen to these:

> 'Reduced stock levels by 17.5 per cent, thereby releasing £210,000 into company cash flow.'

'Assisted in clients' understanding of VAT regulations thus improving customer relations.'

'Improved debt collection time from 85 to 54 days thus ensuring maximum cash flow.'

I'm sure you get the principle.

On pages 72–4 there are some 'Action words' to help you identify your achievements. Think about a job you have held, and put an 'I' in front of each action word to see if it triggers an achievement. Not all the words will generate achievements but a significant proportion should do so.

You can find more illustrations of achievements in the CV examples towards the end of the book.

CHAPTER 25

Use the Past for the Future

Wherever possible, use the immediate past tense or 'aorist' form of the verb to introduce an achievement. The noun form, the infinitive or participle is not as powerful. (Don't worry, this is a book about CVs, not English grammar.)

Here are some examples:

'Managed' rather than 'the management'
'Improved' rather than 'the improvement'
'Investigated' rather than 'the investigation'

The past tense rather than the present participle:

'Designed' rather than 'designing'
'Analyzed' rather than 'analyzing'
'Directed' rather than 'directing'

The past tense rather than the infinitive:

'Secured' rather than 'to secure'
'Organized' rather than 'to organize'
'Captured' rather than 'to capture'

The past tense gives the impression that you have actually done something. It is completed, it is finished, it is achieved – which on a CV is the impression you want to create.

OTHER GRAMMAR GRABBERS

No 'I's
Avoid the first person singular. Save it for the interview. Too much of the first person singular on paper makes you look like a megalomaniac.

Lose the articles
Drop the 'a', 'an' and 'the' from your CV. Organized sales territories is far more punchy than 'organized the sales territories'.

Keep the same tense
The recipient of your CV will get stressed if you keep switching the tense you have used.

Abbreviations
If your reader is unlikely to understand FBs, MISOG and ATOs, then don't use them. IT geeks please ignore this suggestion and use as many as you can. It will mesmerize the HR guy and cause just the right amount of curiosity in your potential operational boss.

Just two more things on achievements before we move on.

Deleting the first person 'I' makes it easier for you to give yourself proper credit without appearing over-boastful.

By using the past tense you don't have to keep using

'I' because you can leave it out and replace it with an asterisk or star. The second point is that you can now indent your achievements on the page so that they stand out better and the eye of the reader is drawn towards them.

Here is an example:

Project Editor   Scholastic Digest   1999 – Present

Scholastic Digest is the largest publisher of scholastic material in the UK. My position was to manage the production of texts, magazines and multimedia instructional programs for the sixth-form market. Main achievements:

- Achieved product goals through supervision of staff ranging from 12 to 23 on projects up to £350,000, including independent copywriters and freelance editors.
- Conducted workshops for teachers so that . . .
- Won the Miller education prize for . . .

Note here the order, job then company then employment dates. There is a brief description of the job followed by the achievements which are indented and the 'I' has been omitted from them as well.

ACTION WORDS

ACHIEVED	APPOINTED	AUDITED
ACQUIRED	APPRAISED	AUGMENTED
ADMINISTERED	APPROVED	AVERTED
ADVISED	ARRANGED	AVOIDED
ANALYSED	ATTAINED	BOUGHT
ANTICIPATED	ASSESSED	BUILT

CAPTURED	FORECAST	ORGANIZED
CENTRALIZED	FORMED	ORIGINATED
COMBINED	FORMULATED	PERFORMED
COMPLETED	GENERATED	PIONEERED
COMPOSED	GUIDED	PLANNED
CONCEIVED	HIRED	POSITIONED
CONTROLLED	IMPLEMENTED	PREPARED
CONVERTED	IMPROVED	PRESENTED
CO-ORIGINATED	IMPROVISED	PREVENTED
CORRECTED	INCREASED	PROCESSED
COUNSELLED	INITIATED	PROCURED
CREATED	INSPIRED	PRODUCED
DECREASED	INSPECTED	PROMOTED
DEFINED	INSTIGATED	PROVED
DEMONSTRATED	INSTRUCTED	PROVIDED
DESIGNED	INSURED	PUBLISHED
DETERMINED	INTERPRETED	PURCHASED
DEVELOPED	INTERVIEWED	RECOMMENDED
DEVISED	INTRODUCED	RECRUITED
DIRECTED	INVENTED	RECTIFIED
DOCUMENTED	INVESTIGATED	RE-DESIGNED
DOUBLED	LAUNCHED	REDUCED
EDITED	LEAD	REGULATED
EFFECTED	LIAISED	REJECTED
ELIMINATED	LIGHTENED	RELATED
EMPLOYED	LIQUIDATED	REMEDIED
ENFORCED	MAINTAINED	REORGANIZED
ENGINEERED	MANAGED	RESEARCHED
ENSURED	MARKETED	RESOLVED
ESTABLISHED	MODERNIZED	REVAMPED
ESTIMATED	MONITORED	REVIEWED
EVALUATED	NEGOTIATED	REVISED
EXCEEDED	OBTAINED	REVITALIZED
EXECUTED	OPERATED	SAVED
EXTRACTED	ORDERED	SCHEDULED

SECURED	STREAMLINED	TIGHTENED
SELECTED	STUDIED	TRADED
SIMPLIFIED	SUPERVISED	TRAINED
SOLD	SUPPORTED	TRANSLATED
SOLVED	SURPASSED	TRIPLED
SPECIFIED	SURVEYED	UTILIZED
STAFFED	TAUGHT	VITALIZED
STANDARDIZED	TERMINATED	WROTE
STIMULATED	TESTED	

A possible activity for you is to go through all these words and put the word 'I' in front. Suddenly you will remember what you did and then, hey presto, you have added another achievement to your list.

CHAPTER 26

Rank Order

Having used the FAB and 'ed's, we are in a position to list our achievements. Well, not quite. Just one more point, and it is another strategy that comes straight from sales.

A rhyming couplet that all good salesmen know is this:

If I can see the world through John Smith's eyes,
I can sell John Smith what John Smith buys

WRITE FOR THE READER

Apply this principle to your list of achievements. Looking at the list of all the things you have done, which do you think Mr Smith, the recruiter, would like to see first, second, third, etc? For example, as an advertising accounts executive you might be most proud of your creative copywriting skills and thus at the top of your achievement list is:

Created concepts and wrote copy for . . .

But the job centres around good client management. This is what Mr John Smith is looking for.

So you should lead with:

Successfully planned promotions for blue-chip clients

before giving any information about how creative your copywriting can be.

In rank ordering your achievements, always write for the reader, your John Smith recruiter, and not for yourself.

CHAPTER 27

Tell Them What They Want To Know

Next important principle: Include only relevant information. If something does not support your career goal, then think hard about including it. Let me give you a personal example. I now work as a Chartered Psychologist with organizations large and small, mainly working with clients on the resolution of management problems. My first job on leaving school was working in a gin factory in Stratford, London E15, stacking bottles of wine. My second job was working as a lift-man in a treacle factory on the Barking Creek in East Ham. My third was as a kitchen hand in Plaistow, again in London. Now on my CV this information would be true, it might even be interesting, but it definitely would not be helpful.

RELEVANT INFORMATION ONLY

My CV therefore would say:

> Prior to 19xx a variety of junior positions in wine distribution, food manufacture and hospitality industries.

I have only included relevant information.

We have seen CVs where people have given their Social Security number, their passport number, medical card number – all irrelevant.

LEAVE THE CHILDREN UNTIL LATER

Frequently on CVs one sees the full names of their children, dates of birth and where they were born. When we challenged the writer of such a CV he justified himself by saying: 'But wait, the employer needed to know all this' – the answer is 'yes', but *not* at the CV stage. Remember the maxim – only enough information to get you the interview.

CHAPTER 28

Kids' Ages

Whilst talking about children – and this goes for men as well as women – if your children are at the ages 5, 8, 10, 11, 13, 15 or 17, all those ages will ring alarm bells in the recruiter's mind because they are critical if a move or relocation to the new job is called for. The best place to explain what you are going to do about your children's education is at interview and then only if it is raised by the interviewer.

GROWN UP CHILDREN

Also, if your age is outside the 'golden decade' don't say you have two adult children aged 25 and 27; it just emphasizes your age again. The recruiter who is just the gatekeeper might think to herself before she has even seen you 'Goodness, this person has children who are older than me.'

CHAPTER 29

No Jokes Please, Recruitment is Serious

Many people try to liven up the selector's day by injecting humour into their CVs. Don't be tempted. Don't be cute, chatty or funny. Selection and recruitment is a serious business. To be in the recruitment business is to be in a risk averse business like law or accounting – when it is easier for a recruiter to say 'No' than 'Yes', he or she usually says 'No'. By and large, recruiters always say 'No' to humour. Not because they are boring people but because their own jobs depend on how successful they are at picking the right people. What do you think happens to recruiters who keep selecting the wrong people? They join the job market very quickly.

It is hard enough to be funny in person, let alone on paper.

MISFIRED HUMOUR

Here are some samples from people who have tried to be funny on their CVs. Under interests:

'Golf, golf and more golf'

Now, I'm personally not a golfer so I'm not too impressed by that. Under reasons for leaving a job:

'To keep up with the school fees'

Now, if I have strong views about equality and the benefits of state education, this is not going to find very much favour. Under main achievements:

'Wrestling with machine codes and winning'

If I'm looking for a programmer, I would expect this anyway.

Basic rule: Don't try to be funny. Your CV should be serious if you want your application to be taken seriously.

CHAPTER 30

Reasons for Leaving

Even in these days there is still an implicit understanding that people want and employers can provide lifetime employment. Maybe it is a hangover from the bygone age of the fifties and sixties when once you were employed by an organization you were there for life. Job hopping now as then was not thought to be good; it hints at instability.

THE FOUR REASONS FOR LEAVING

Consequently, it is better not to include reasons for leaving on your CV. Such information can only serve to remind the potential employer that you are in control of your career rather than vice versa. Also, there are basically only four reasons why people leave jobs – better prospects, more pay, relocation or they were fired. Any of them, if the employer thinks about them seriously, makes you a potential risk as an employee – the question 'will you stay' is raised by the first three and the last will almost guarantee you stay unemployed. It is better to leave such things to be explained during the interview, than to try to justify your career moves at the CV stage.

Welcome to Niles District Library!
www.nileslibrary.com
269-683-8545
You checked out the following items:

1. Perfect CV
   Barcode: 33007000064960
   Due: 2/3/14 11:59 PM
2. The world almanac for kids 2014
   Barcode: 33008120102458
   Due: 2/3/14 11:59 PM
3. The Marvel Comics encyclopedia :
   Barcode: 33008120118132
   Due: 2/3/14 11:59 PM

NDL-1 2014-01-13 19:10

HOW NOT TO GET AN INTERVIEW

The worst case we ever saw was on a CV that ran:

> REASONS FOR LEAVING: Dismissed: Due to personality clash with boss: Currently taking this employer to an Industrial Tribunal: Confident of winning.

He came to us wondering why his CV was not producing any interviews!

The advice is, leave out 'Reasons for leaving' from your CV. Explain it later in the selection process and then only on a specific invitation to do so by the interviewer.

CHAPTER 31

Early Mistakes

If you were once a junior secretary and are now a Director of Advertising or Human Resources Manager, it is not going to be helpful to put your early job on your CV. If you were a lab technician before you became an accountant, or took your law degree part time whilst working as a janitor, it just does not help to include the more humble positions.

RECENT JOBS ONLY

Most employers are mainly interested in what you have been doing recently. What you did ten years ago is unlikely to make a significant contribution to your next job. So where appropriate use summary statements such as 'Prior to 19— a variety of junior jobs in engineering and retailing'. Note we mention the industries sector not the job titles.

Sometimes a previous job is directly useful and then it should be included: a meat buyer who was once a butcher, for example, or a nurse who is now a Unit General Manager are obvious examples of relevant experience. It was once said that the British car industry began to fail when accountants were appointed to run them rather than engineers who had shop floor experience.

You will have to decide for yourself how best to account for the early years of your career on your CV. The basic question to ask is: does it fit and/or support my present career aspirations? If it does not help you in any way, then it should be omitted.

CHAPTER 32

Education

Your education successes should be set out employing the same principles as in the career section. Please do not make your employer hack through all your GCSEs if you have a degree or higher qualification. Consequently, the reverse chronological rule applies just as much to education as it does to your career.

OBSOLETE DEGREES

In the same way your qualification is more important than where it was gained, which is more important again than when it was achieved. The number of CVs where the date of the qualification is given first is quite amazing. For those outside the 'golden decade' (see pages 25–26), this can only accentuate your age – 'Gosh, this person was at university before I was born!' Also, in today's world of rapid change most science degrees are obsolete in terms of usable knowledge after about a decade. What is being sold is not the things you know about but the intellectual, conceptual and analytical abilities which you demonstrated in order to gain the qualification.

THE 'TOPSY CURVE'

What frequently occurs up to the age of 30 is what is called the 'Topsy CV', because it just grew. This is a graduate CV which was written on leaving university and then subsequently added to prior to each job move. Thus a 'Topsy CV' gives as much weight to the final year project at university or college as it does to the achievements of the last job. With a little thought it becomes obvious that newly qualified job seekers need to provide lots of information about their studies because they have nothing else to offer. Once someone has had some work experience the emphasis must shift to this area. Employers, except in academia and not always then, are more interested in what you can do for them than how well qualified you are. Sometimes this is difficult for the highly qualified to accept. Just ask yourself the question 'If I was about to be treated in an emergency, who would I prefer to undertake the operation – a recently qualified surgeon who had not performed the operation before, or a paramedic who had successfully completed the procedure many times?' The latter, of course. Ideally one would like qualifications together with the successful experience but given a choice, experience wins every time.

RESISTING AN EDUCATION

This is why those without formal tertiary qualifications, if they have been successful in their careers, should not worry about not having degrees and diplomas. Employers prefer experience. Yes, of course, there are the professions where formal qualifications are a prerequisite for a job, but in the wide world of work, professional jobs are a small fraction of the total. In fact, although I would not recommend this as an excuse not to gain qualifications, most entrepreneurs from Alan Sugar to Richard Branson to the late Robert Maxwell seem to do rather well without the more traditional formal qualifications. Sometimes, it takes a good brain to resist an education!

To return again to your qualifications, your GCSEs, A' levels or the courses you did at college. If you are pursuing a career in the sciences do not list your GCSEs thus:

English, English Literature, History, French, Geography, Maths, Chemistry and Physics

It is not as impressive as:

Maths, Physics, Chemistry, etc.

The same principle can be applied to topics and projects at college – lead with the most appropriate first.

CHAPTER 33

Health

Should you tell your prospective employer about your state of health? You could take the view that how healthy you are is your own private concern. But it is obvious that the employer wants employees who are at work rather than off work with some malady and drawing sick pay. Consequently, if you are healthy, say so, for it can only be in your favour. 'Excellent' is the word which most frequently appears on CVs, though I am not sure of the difference between good health and excellent health.

If your health has not been good then my advice is not to say so on the CV. The fact that you are returning to work must mean that you are currently fit for work, but this is the sort of information which is far better discussed at interview. If I have two candidates whose CVs offer the same skills and experience, but one candidate confesses a significant health problem from which he has fully recovered and the other does not (although he too suffered from the same illness), it is obvious which one will be given preference for the interview.

AN ILLUSION OF GOOD HEALTH

A way of creating the illusion of good health is to include some reference to a sporting activity among your interests and, if possible, a sporting achievement, no matter how long ago. It shows that you were fit and healthy at one time in your life with the implication that you are still fit now.

Employers are, for obvious reasons, biased against the weak and the sick, no matter how fit they are now. The best place to justify your fitness for the job is at the interview, not at the CV stage. So if you are healthy say so; if not, then omit this information.

WHERE DISABILITY IS A PLUS

The exception is if you are registered disabled. In my experience employers positively discriminate in favour of those who used to be called 'green card carriers'. If your disability does not have a direct bearing on your job, then it is almost a guarantee of an interview.

If you have an obvious disability my advice would be, whether or not you declared it on your CV, to advise your potential employer before you go for the interview. If you attend interviews in a wheelchair or have a false limb and this has not been mentioned on the CV it is likely that you will be remembered for your disability rather than the skills and experience you can bring to the job irrespective of your suitability.

CHAPTER 34

Gimmick CVs

Do not be tempted to use gimmicks. If your CV needs a special gimmick to gain attention, rather than your achievements or skills, then although your CV will be noticed it will not pass closer scrutiny.

If your CV is markedly different in paper colour or typeface it says quietly, 'I'm an outsider trying to get in.' A gimmick CV gives the same message even more clearly.

THE CV AND THE RAIL PASS

Successful exceptions are few. A gimmick CV that worked was for a traineeship in the creative department of a famous PR and advertising company. Here the applicant did a one-page CV, had it miniaturized and gummed to the back of a weekly rail travel pass, and sent it with a one-line covering letter which read,

Look what you can have if you fund one of these each week.

It gained an interview and the job. An Asian graduate trainee wrote off to all the recruiters that were visiting his university offering himself as an Indian take-away with his qualification, skills and experience set out like a menu for an Indian meal. Again, this worked, but by and large gimmick CVs provide a little welcome humour and diversion in the recruiter's humdrum day and little else. Would you buy a car because of flashing lights in the show window or select a restaurant for a celebration dinner because of the chance of winning a weekend break away? Like you, employers are essentially traditional and sensible in their buying habits and not influenced by the superficial. Keep your CV normal.

DISK CV

If you want a computing job in a small or high-tech company putting your CV on a disk used to be a popular approach which began, like so many of these things, in the US. However, since the advent of computer viruses many firms have strict policies about the use of floppies when their pedigree and form are unknown.

WEB PAGE CV

Because of the advances in search engine technology many employers now search the web for potential employees.

If you are not up to this you can hire a web master who will do one for you. A word of warning if you are going to do this you must do it well. Look naf and you will get a naf result.

The usual rules apply:

Less is more
It has to look professional
Keep it simple
Make it customer friendly

There are many career sites which will invite you to register your CV on their site. Their instructions are usually luddite proof so you should have no difficulty. Do not be encouraged to duplicate their CV structure for your own hard copy CV. For the most part, for some reason their CV structures are very old fashioned and you will not be doing yourself any favours if you duplicate them for your personal hardcopy.

CHAPTER 35

Coping with Bias

Recruitment is unfair. Yes, there is some legislation designed to minimize discrimination against applicants for reasons of sex, race, colour or creed but a lot of prejudices still exist.

The basic rule is to put any information which ignorant, prejudiced people will use against you on the back page. If you are not British don't put your nationality immediately after your name and address. It just does not help. If you have a foreign sounding name yet you look British, then use a photograph irrespective of my advice on page 38.

CHANGING YOUR NAME

I worked with a beautiful and brilliant Ethiopian woman who graduated from Oxford University with a good honours degree. She was fluent in English, French and Italian as well as several dialects of her homeland. The facts are these. She sent 150 CVs to graduate recruiters and had no invitations to interview. She anglicized her name and remailed the 150 CVs and achieved 10 interviews. There were only two variables – her name and the time she sent her CV.

In the UK you can choose to call yourself by any name you wish providing it is not your intention to defraud. Maybe John Smith and Fred Bloggs are having a hard time and a zero response from their CVs which they are circulating in Ethiopia.

THE VEXED QUESTION OF MARITAL STATUS

We were recently working as consultants with a young woman who held very strong feminist views, she objected to putting her marital status on her CV. In the end we persuaded her to do 50 CVs with her status and 50 without. I regret to report that it was the latter that generated more interviews. We have repeated the experiment several times since and achieved the same response.

Now standby for some real sexism. We repeated this experiment with males and, guess what, it was reversed!! So the rule now is:

If you're male include your marital status
If you're female omit your marital status

If selectors are silly enough to be prejudiced then you can be wise enough not to play their silly games.

It is a difficult decision. If one has to go to these lengths to get a job with a company, would you really want to work for that company anyway?

CHAPTER 36

What to Leave Out

As the CV will form the basis of the interview, and negative information at interview always attracts more supplementary and probing questions, your CV should contain only that which is positive about you. So here is a section about what you might like to leave out. Of course, you must be prepared to answer questions in these areas at interview, but at the CV stage your maxim should be:

'Yours to know and theirs to find out.'

AVOIDING PREJUDICE

Remember that each of us at a basic level is biased. Birds of a feather flock together and recruiters are no different from the rest. They like to recruit in their own image. Most recruiters in the UK are WASPS – that is, white, Anglo-Saxon and Protestant. They are also married with 2.3 children, living in suburbia and able to buy their clothes from M&S. If you are different in any way from the norm then the sorry fact of life is that you will experience prejudice at the CV paper sort. Things are, fortunately, changing but we have not yet had many prime ministers with few O levels who spend some of their years in Brixton. If it is a fact that recruiters are biased then do not give them the opportunity to exercise this inadequacy at the CV sort stage. Any information which can give rise to bias should be left out. It is an indictment of our present society but if you are single, black, an ex-shop steward who failed your Bar finals at the first attempt and spent five years 15 years ago working for London Transport, are politically active, jailed for civil disobedience and have dual Nigerian/UK citizenship your chances of getting to interview for a typical law job if you include this information are slim, irrespective of how brilliant your career and achievements may be.

SUGGESTED OMISSIONS

Here are some things you might like to consider omitting:

(Those marked with an asterisk* are dealt with specifically elsewhere in the book.)

- Examinations you have failed
- Your health, if poor*
- Major illness, both physical and mental*
- Junior jobs irrelevant to your present career thrust*
- Employment of less than a year
- Reason for leaving employment*
- Dates of qualifications
- Ages of children*
- Marital Status – if female* – if gay – if single, male and over 30
- Children, if adult*

- Period(s) of state detention
- Past Trade Union status – unless you are going for a job in industrial relations with a Union or into politics
- Dangerous or 'different' interests, e.g., hand-gliding and bungee jumping*
- Nationality if not British – securing work permits is extra unwanted and difficult work for employers
- Political affiliations
- Place of birth if not in UK
- Fluency in languages of no direct use within the Western world or to the job on offer
- Higher qualifications if the jobs for which you are applying have no need of them
- Your current salary and benefits*
- Your anticipated salary and benefits*
- Your photograph*
- Your referees*
- Your career ambitions/objectives unless you are a recent graduate
- Anything that makes you look extreme or different

CHAPTER 37

But I've Already Sent Out My CV to Lots of Employers

Do not worry if you have bought this book after sending out your CV, because CVs have a shelf life of at most about two weeks in the mind of recruiters. Your CV might get put in the potential candidates file but either way you can always send it again on the pretext of having updated the document for the employer. Many a time in my experience an employer has seen a candidate on the 'new improved' CV whereas there was a nil response to the original document.

CV Don'ts – Again

- Do not lie
- Do not list current salary
- Do not state your salary requirements
- Do not give reasons for leaving your previous job
- Do not use 'I' unless absolutely necessary
- Do not bind your CV
- Do not use unfamiliar facts, abbreviations or job titles
- Do not include a photograph
- Do not have any spelling errors
- Do not have any grammatical errors
- Do not use coloured paper
- Do not use graphics
- Do not be humorous
- Do not send photocopies
- Do not have more than four pages of A4
- Do not go back more than 15 years in your career
- Do not include addresses of previous employers
- Do not give referees or references
- Do not use a chronological format
- Do not present your CV on anything else but A4 paper
- Do not include too many in-house training courses

- Do not over hype your CV
- Do not make hand written changes
- Do not leave unexplained gaps in your CV
- Do not be long-winded
- Do not use long words or long sentences
- Do not claim skills that are not reflected in your achievements
- Do not use boy scout words or language
- Do not date your CV
- Do not include a career objective
- Do not state round figures in your achievements
- Do not use self-congratulatory language
- Do not send your CV to box numbers that do not also provide the name the Company
- Do not declare strange or dangerous interests
- Do not send your CV to 'Dear Sir' or 'Madam'
- Do not include a logo, clipart or if you privileged enough to have one, your family crest
- Do not use a secretarial service to structure your CV
- Do not send it to the HR Department when it is a cold application

Please note: These are all general 'don'ts' and all have exceptions that prove the rule.

CHAPTER 39

Application Forms

You will find it very frustrating if having spent hours on crafting your CV and sending it off with the perfect covering letter, the only reward for your labours is an application form.

Whilst this may be frustrating, remember two things. First, not everyone gets an application form so your CV has done its job. Second, no application form I have yet seen gives the applicant scope to write everything that is appropriate. This means your CV can still play its important role in gaining the interview.

HOW RECRUITERS USE THEM

Employers use application forms rather like the army uses uniforms – they position everyone. It is easier for recruiters to interview from an application form because they know where to look for what they want, whether it be experience, personal details or expertise. It is helpful when you are trying to keep up the rapport to be able to glance down to a certain position and know that that section on the form will give the required information. Hacking through a CV at interview mitigates against rapport and a natural flow to the conversation.

FOR FURTHER INFORMATION . . .

Employers will not shortlist you if you return the application form over which you have printed, however neatly, 'Please see CV'. You must complete the form: but in doing so you can write at the bottom of various sections particularly those detailing experience and achievements 'For further information please see my CV', which, of course, you have enclosed. (Please do not expect employers to have kept your previous CV or documentation.) It is no guarantee that your CV will be read again but you have given it your best shot.

CHAPTER 40

What Next?

Once the CV has been written it must find its way to as many appropriate desks as possible. It is surprising that so many people spend ages constructing their CV and then don't send it to anyone, as if the invitations to interview are supposed to come by some form of osmosis.

LEARNING TO 'PYRAMID'

To whom should you send your CV? Here you have to learn to pyramid – as in pyramid sales. Your CV needs to go to someone who:

1. Can offer you a job
2. Refer you to someone who can offer you a job
3. Can tell you of a job opening
4. Refer you to someone who can suggest a potential job
5. Can give you the name of someone who can do any of the above

THERE IS NO LIMIT

Getting a job is a process of being turned down. Getting an interview is about telling as many people as possible that you are looking for the next stage in your career. If your CV stays on your desk at home, so will your career.

CHAPTER 41

Who Can Give You a Job

'Spend as much time as you can with prospective customers' is a basic rule of sales. Salesmen who spend all their time at their desk writing reports, talking to their design and manufacturing people and generally staying in-house are unlikely to be successful because none of those people are likely to buy their product. It is the same for the job hunter – who is going to give you a job? It is not:

Family – they can give you support

or

Friends – they can maybe tell you of openings

or

Agencies – they can only submit your details on your behalf

or

HR Departments – they can only shortlist you.

It is only decision makers in appropriate firms that can give you the job you want.

PICKING UP THE £50 NOTES

If an eccentric millionaire passed you on the street scattering handfuls of £50, £20, £10 and £5 notes there would soon be lots of people, including yourself, picking up the paper money. The best strategy would be not to pick up as many notes as possible but to collect as many of the high denominations as you could. In this way you would maximize the gains. Job search should follow the same principles. Most people just write to agencies then sit back and complain that:

a) they have heard nothing
b) agencies and head hunters are hopeless
c) agencies cannot understand your technical expertise

(although the latter might make you feel good when you have just had your ego dented by needing to change jobs). It is only employers who can give someone a job, so they are the equivalent of the £50 notes. Of course, your letter will be regarded as junk mail by most of them but you are more likely to be successful here than working with the other categories (the lower denominations in cash terms).

John Courtis, who runs his own excellent head hunting firm, sends a standard letter to job searchers – it makes the point so well that I have set it out in full on page 141.

The moral is simple: *Spend most of your energy contacting the most likely employers.*

CHAPTER 42

Covering Letter

Remember the sum on page 12. Not only does it apply to the CV but also to the covering letter. In fact more so, because the covering letter is the packaging for the CV. If the letter does not command the attention of the selector then why should he or she go on to read the CV?

Here are some obvious basics.

First, where possible it should be typed. Most written business communications are typed; if your letter is not you are signalling quite clearly to your future employer that you are an outsider trying to get in.

DON'T SPLIT THE INFINITIVES!

Of course spelling and grammar should both be correct. Split infinitives still annoy people. You must remember that at this stage in the selection process it is only your letter and CV that contain information about you and who wants an employee who cannot even present him or herself correctly?

I would suggest that you do not right-hand justify your letter. As with the CV, it gives the impression that this is a standard document (which, of course, it is) that you have sent off to hundreds of potential employers (which, of course, you have).

See Chapter 44 for further advice on letters.

CHAPTER 43

To Whom?

It is always best to write cold to your potential employer. In our consultancy, where we help thousands of people every year get jobs, something like 84% of the people we work with get jobs in what is called the Hidden Jobs Market (HJM). The HJM is just a fancy way of saying writing cold or writing direct. Here is the way:

1. If you respond to an advert you could be one applicant out of 200 or even more. If you write direct you are the only one in the frame.

2. If you apply to an advert you have five jumps to get that job.

   First jump get you accepted by the agency
   Second jump gets you short-listed by the agency
   Third jump gets you to the firm's HR department
   Forth jump gets you short-listed by HR
   Fifth jump gets you the offer from the line manager

   If you write directly to your potential boss's boss you only have one jump.

3. Agencies charge the organization anywhere up to 33 per cent of first year's salary. If you apply direct you come free and that makes you even more attractive.

4. Advertising is very expensive for the organization. If you apply direct again you come free.

5. HR Department at best can only say 'Maybe'. When you apply direct the line Manager is the person who can say 'Yes'.

6. Behind every job advert there is a job description drawn up by HR and you have to fit it. If you apply direct the job description can be written around you.

7. By the time the job is in HR's hands it has been salary banded. If you apply direct you have more chance to negotiate your starting rate in the direction you would like.

8. If you apply to HR they don't always know what is happening in the near future. If you apply direct the Line Manager will know who is retiring, who is pregnant, who he or she wants to fire or transfer, what part of the department needs additional manpower.

9. Applying direct makes you look more of a self-starter.

Sometimes people we work with find this difficult and say things like 'But isn't my letter just so much like junk mail?' and we reply 'Yes, and have you ever in the whole of you life bought something or know someone who bought something from junk mail?' The point being that junk mail goes through a metamorphosis when there is a need. So will your application.

SEND IT TO A PERSON

Your letter must go to a named person. 'Dear Sir/Madam' is an insult. Until you secure the interview your letter has the status of junk mail. If you begin 'Dear Sir/Madam' it is more likely to be treated as such, and will probably not even reach the decision maker. Secretaries are paid to file junk or unsolicited mail vertically under W.B. If the Reader's Digest can reach you by name and personalize the correspondence, you can do the same, so write directly to the likely decision maker by name.

FINDING THE RIGHT NAME

The decision maker is likely to be your potential boss's boss. It is usually quite easy to find out the name of the appropriate recipient just by telephoning the receptionist. Some organizations, like banks, pharmaceutical companies and defence organizations have policies about not giving information over the telephone, in which case go to one of the directories (in any reference library), find the appropriate director and ask them or their secretary. Tell them that you want to send some information to the person responsible for the xyz function, would it be the director (or his/her secretary) to whom you are speaking? This usually prompts a 'No' and that it should go to Mr or Ms so-and-so.

If you are a director or a senior executive then write to the Chief Executive by name. They are probably inundated with unsolicited mail from job hunters but if you have a skill profile which might be useful they will respond appropriately. The letters on pages 138 and 139 are real examples and proof that the system works.

THE HR DEPARTMENT

Giving you this advice will alienate my friends in human resources departments. Being responsible for recruitment and selection, they naturally expect all job hunters' correspondence to be directed to them. However, good and professional as they are, HR departments are but gatekeepers, albeit important gatekeepers, in the selection process. HR selectors can only say 'No', they cannot say 'Yes'. It would not be fair to talk about monkeys and organ grinders, buttons and shirts or oily rags and engineers, but the principle is the same. It is only if you want a job in human resources that you should write to that department, important though it is. Always write to the person who can give you a job.

COVERING LETTERS

CHAPTER 44

Structure of the Covering Letter

The purpose of the covering letter is very simple: it is to get the recipient to read your CV – no more, no less. Although this is obvious and simplistic, it is surprising how many covering letters:

- Are too long
- Repeat the content of the CV
- Are written from the applicant's point of view
- Contain negative information

and besides all this contain spelling and grammatical errors.

To my mind and in my experience, the covering letter needs only three paragraphs.

1st Paragraph From the recipient's viewpoint or benefit give your reason for writing.

A good way of ensuring this is to use the sales strategy letter of beginning this paragraph with the word 'Your'.

For example:

- 'Your advertisement was of great interest . . .'
- 'Your company enjoys an excellent reputation in engineering . . .'

- 'Your article in *Business Week* . . .'
- 'Your recent results . . .'

Employers are bound to be interested in what is happening from their viewpoint.

2nd Paragraph To customize your CV and direct the reader to some unique selling point which meets or hits a specific need of the potential employer.

For example:

- 'You will see from my enclosed CV . . .'
- 'Customer Services has been the main thrust of my career . . .'
- 'Last year I won the largest widget order in the North East . . .'
- 'Being a Unix specialist who is fluent in German . . .'

3rd Paragraph This is to ask for the interview, but remember interviews are work for HR people. So we translate this into 'discussion' or 'meeting'.

For example:

- 'The opportunity of a discussion . . .'
- 'The chance to meet with you . . .'

Finally, this third paragraph is to prompt the reader into some form of action, thus:

- 'I look forward to hearing from you'

or, if you are applying for jobs where some degree of confidence and assertiveness is required or expected:

- 'Perhaps I may telephone your office next week to see how you may wish to progress the matter . . .'

You will notice that this is the first and only place where tentative language is used, 'Perhaps I may . . . to see how you may wish . . .' This just takes the aggressive edge off the intention. For the most part, with cold letters your call will not be welcome but in today's climate no one will think ill of you if you work hard at getting a job. Remember, if there is a potential position for you your call will be welcome.

You will find examples of how to end your letter in Chapter 45.

What follows are some tips and strategies and what not to do in the Covering Letter and some suggestions as to how they could be improved. We begin with three examples of what not to do.

EXAMPLE 1 – WHAT NOT TO DO

16 Quartz Close
Woosehill
Wokingham
Berkshire
RG11 9TS

26 May 2002

Dear Sir/Madam,

I have seen your advertisements in various publications and feel that you are ideally placed to help me further my career.

I am an experienced Computer Customer Service Professional, and I currently work for one of the leading companies in the field. I am looking to expand my experience by moving to another company.

I would welcome an opportunity to discuss my experience and any potential opportunities with you. I will call you next week.

Yours sincerely,

Mr P. I. Maxin

Comments
From someone who is in customer service this is dreadful. Here are some of the errors:

1. 'Dear Sir/Madam' – This is almost saying, 'I don't care who you are and I'm too lazy to find out.'
2. Every sentence begins with 'I' – the writer sounds like an egomaniac.
3. The whole letter is written from the viewpoint of what the potential employer can do for the applicant. In retailing terms this letter is almost the equivalent of a shopkeeper putting up a sign in his window saying, 'Shop here so I can make a profit on you.'
4. 'I will call you next week' – There is a difference between assertiveness which is essential in getting a job these days and naked aggression. This bald statement is just rude!
5. 'Yours sincerely' – You must get this right. Dear Sir demands a 'Yours faithfully'. Only when writing to a specifically named person is 'Yours sincerely' appropriate.
6. 'Mr P. I. Maxin' – he *must* be an egoist. It is not customary to put the appellation Mr (or Ms, Mrs etc.) in front of your name. If you must do it, then put it after your name in brackets.

EXAMPLE 2 – AGAIN, WHAT NOT TO DO

Dear

I write in reference to our recent telephone conversation.

I enclose my CV for your consideration. I am aware that its presentation is not ideal and I am working on an improved format.

I have enjoyed a successful career in Engineering, including management, training, counselling and sales/marketing activities.

I am interested in the possibility of becoming an associate in such fields as . . .

Comments
This was a letter sent to our consultancy. It was handwritten and was not at all easy to read.

1. Ideally your covering letter should enjoy the same style and typeface as your CV. If this is not possible then do try to have it typed. If it is handwritten, since most of the world of work communicates on paper by the typed word, your letter signals clearly that you are an outsider trying to get in.
2. 'I am aware that [my CV] is not ideal' – This is amazing! What is the implication here?

   – I can't be bothered to update it
   – You are not worth the effort of the rewrite
   – This application is less important than other things I have to do

It would have been better not to allude to the paucity of the CV than include this statement.

3. 'I have enjoyed a successful career' – implications of this should be thoroughly thought through. This phrase implies to me that the writer is now retired and no longer making a positive or significant contribution.

4. ' . . . in the possibility of . . . in such fields as . . .' Instructions on how to write sales letters make a significant point about tentative language. In covering letters it makes you sound unsure or uncertain. Phrases and words such as the following might usefully be omitted:
   - I feel
   - I think
   - I might
   - Perhaps
   - Only
   - Just
   - It may

Unless, of course, you deliberately wish to appear tentative (see comment number 4 in Example 1).

EXAMPLE 3 – THIS IS THE WORST EXAMPLE

Dear Mr

Here are five reasons why you should employ me:

1. If you do not, one of your competitors will.
2. Leadership qualities, both verbally and by example.
3. A refusal to accept second-best in life.
4. Major achievements, mostly in the future.
5. In possession of a healthy body and a healthy mind.

Comments
In fact, the original had 11 reasons and the above represents an abbreviated version. There is nothing wrong in making your covering letter different or being assertive or pushy but this is just silly, coming as it does from an MBA graduate. Even the points are open to question, for example:

- What is a verbal leader?
- How can you sell future achievements if you have no track record?
- Employers take as read that employees are healthy.

This list could be offered by most applicants. There is little which is unique here. If you wish to try this approach, which sometimes works, then a strong client orientation, coupled with creative and individual uniqueness is a must.

THIS IS THE MOST IDOSYNCRATIC COVERING LETTER

Dear Sir

My name is John Smith, I am 47 and live in Balmain.

Previous to unemployment I was self-employed for 30 years. In that time I employed many men of different trades around the waterside, including painters and dockers. My business closed because the Taxation Department caused me to sell my factory. After which the bank decided I did not have enough capital and forced me into selling the family home. This has caused great hostility within me towards government and banking.

I have back problems, asbestosis and emphysema and I find taking orders difficult and I lose my temper easily. My principles are family then honour and honesty.

My criminal record includes numerous driving offences, deliberate damage to private property, resisting arrest, assault, assault with grievous bodily harm and possession of an unlicensed pistol.

My interests are fishing, bowling, family socializing, short stories and boxing.

Yours sincerely

John Smith

Whilst this letter may stretch your credibility it is real and it comes from our Sydney offices. The writer does get ten points for honesty but minus ten for naïvety.
 Here are some better examples.

EXAMPLE 4

Dear

Engineering costs are a significant overload. For appropriate control, good management and best manufacturing methods are vital.

May I help in this important area?

My extensive skills and experience cover:

- Engineering management in 'blue-chip' companies
- Planning and executing capital investment programs up to £2.3M
- Reducing labour costs in a Trade Union environment
- Introducing effective machine maintenance

The opportunity to discuss with you how my knowledge and ability could be used to your advantage would be most welcome.

Yours sincerely

Comments
This letter, which was sent cold to possible employers, won an interview and subsequently a job, so the letter did what it was supposed to do.

1. Notice how this letter, in comparison to Example 3, continually has the needs of the employer in mind and uses tentative language in the right place to soften the assertiveness.
2. The letter begins strongly with a statement which every manufacturing company would support.

3. Personally, I would have strengthened the selling points by:
   a) Using the past, e.g., Plann*ed* and execut*ed*
   b) Quantifying the reduction in labour costs and the machine maintenance
   c) Made more of the potential benefits to the employer.

Next is an example of how to present a non-traditional career.

EXAMPLE 5

Dear

What do sweets and lighting have in common?

- BOTH NEED TO DELIVER MAXIMUM CONSUMER SATISFACTION
- BOTH NEED THEIR BENEFITS COMMUNICATED TO THEIR TARGET MARKETS
- BOTH NEED TO GENERATE A SATISFACTORY PROFIT FOR THE COMPANY
- BOTH HAVE BENEFITED FROM MY DIRECTION

As an experienced Marketing Director, I have a proven record in the management of change, resulting in increased customer satisfaction and an improved company profitability. My CV which is enclosed demonstrates this.

I am happy to supply further information or meet for a discussion when examples of my achievements can be matched more closely to situations in your organization.

Yours sincerely

Comments
This is another cold letter to target employers.

1. This job seeker makes an advantage of a career background which is not normal, i.e., from confectionery to lighting products, in an interesting way.
2. The offer of 'examples of my achievements' is also an additional reason why an employer might want to see

you. You obviously have more chance of getting the job even if the interviewer initially only wants to see you because of your 'examples'.

EXAMPLE 6 – LETTER TO HEADHUNTER

Dear

There is a legend that memories only last three months. I contacted you in the summer and am enclosing another copy of my CV to update your records.

I would like to convert this piece of paper into a face and look forward to meeting you.

Yours sincerely,

Comments

This gained several interviews when the first CV, which was written before the writer had advice, achieved a nil response.

1. Headhunters receive hundreds of cold letters a day. They usually begin with a very boring 'I was a senior executive with . . .', so you can see how this effort was refreshingly different.
2. The last paragraph here is really interesting and provocative and I can see why it worked.
3. Most job seekers think that headhunters and agencies have hundreds of jobs on their books – they don't. Yes, they do use their contacts to secure assignments, but most of them do what most job seekers should be doing for themselves: contacting employers direct. My advice is be your own headhunter, representing yourself.

Headhunters, however, receive hundreds of unsolicited letters each week. See the advice of John Courtis in Chapter 47.

EXAMPLE 7 – IN RESPONSE TO AN ADVERT

Dear

The ability to steer the xxx Co. through an increasingly more complex and competitive marketplace.

The experience to understand intimately the requirements and opportunities for commercial sponsorship of the arts.

The stature to lead a prestigious organization and represent the xxx Co. at the highest levels of Industry and Government.

The skills to position the xxx Co. for optimum and profitable success.

The creative sensitivity to balance the artistic and the commercial requirements of the xxx Co.

If my understanding of the requirements for the role of Managing Director of the xxx Co. is correct, then you will find I certainly fit the bill! My attached CV details the bare bones of the success I have built as Managing Director and as President of the Industry Federation.

I look forward to an early opportunity to demonstrate how my particular skills and experience could be used to build and sustain the success of the xxx Co.

Oh yes! I trust that boundless energy and enthusiasm combined with an all-consuming passion for classical music would not count against me?

Yours sincerely

Comments

This was written to a leading orchestra company in response to an advertisement.

1. The writer has attempted to get behind the words of the advert to demonstrate that, although his background is in a totally different arena, he can identify the issues and has the skill and experience to address them.
2. The last line just hints at the disposition of the man behind the letter. (He did not get the job but he got an interview, although there were hundreds of applicants.)
3. In the original letter there was one split infinitive and one typo, but in this case the writer was forgiven.

EXAMPLE 8

Dear Mr

Your paper machine quality control systems and distributed control systems have been formidable competitors to our products in South East Asia and Japan for several years now.

I have for some time been expecting the same competition from your excellent company in Europe and it is interesting to note that you are not more active in the European paper markets than you are.

Should your strategy be entering the European market for paper machine control systems I can be of direct assistance.

As you will see from my attached career résumé I helped establish Accuracy as the leading supplier of quality control systems to the paper industry in Europe and have in-depth knowledge and experience of this market in the UK, France, Holland, Belgium and Germany, as well as being trilingual.

My more recent experience includes the introduction of both the xx and yy Master systems to the paper and other industries.

Mr W. W., President of ZZ Corporation, who is a long-standing friend and colleague from the days when we worked together at BBB, suggests I write to you direct. Perhaps I may telephone you in the next few days to determine when a convenient meeting can be arranged for us to discuss the opportunities which the European

Market presents for you and the start-up assistance I could provide.

I do hope a brief meeting will be possible.

Yours sincerely

Comment
This was a cold letter. It did not gain a job but it did gain for this very able executive a two-week consultancy assignment in Japan.

Do your potential employers' thinking for them. This is an excellent example of an applicant who has done a wonderful job of doing his potential employer's thinking for him and then sold himself as the ideal candidate.

CHAPTER 45

Example Endings

It is surprising how many job hunters have difficulty ending their letters. Here are some examples, all of which come from letters that have won interviews:

- I would be pleased to meet you to discuss how I could contribute to your organization.
- I would welcome the opportunity to discuss with you how my knowledge and ability could be used in your company.
- I hope there might be an opportunity for a personal discussion.
- This letter and my CV provide the basis of my career achievements, but I would be pleased to flesh them out at a personal meeting to see if there is an opportunity to work with your company.
- I am frequently in Cheltenham and can be contacted on 020 7923 3456.
- If you think it would help, I would be delighted to meet you, to talk about this.
- My CV is enclosed. I would welcome a letter or your call to my office.

- I live locally and would be pleased to discuss with you, at any time convenient to yourself, the position advertised or any other that will enable me to provide input and benefit to your organization.
- I attach a note summarizing my background and experience. I should, of course, be glad to come and see you. May I ring to find out if a meeting could be worthwhile?
- A phone call to my office (020 7923 3456) will reach me, or a letter to the above address. My CV is attached. I hope to hear from you.
- My CV is attached and if you would like to see me I should very much like to see you.
- Might not do any harm, at least to talk, if you have a mind to. My CV is enclosed and I hope to hear from you.
- I look forward to your reply and if there are any work areas upon which you require further information do not hesitate to contact me.
- The broadly based interests I have developed would quickly allow me to raise my knowledge to specialist level in a number of fields – a bold statement but one you might be satisfied with if we would meet.
- If I may, I will call your secretary next week to see if it is convenient for me to see you.
- I would like to meet you so that I can elaborate on these bare facts and answer any questions. I look forward to hearing from you.

CHAPTER 46

Do Cold Letters Work?

Put simply – yes when sent to the people who can give you jobs – i.e., Employers. The best analogy I can give is that of oranges: everyone has bought oranges at some time. Greengrocers always display their fruit in the window or outside. Hundreds of people walk by every day and some purchase oranges. However, everybody needs oranges at some time. Job applicants should send out their CVs to anyone who might be able to offer them a job. Just as the greengrocer displays his oranges in front of potential purchasers, you should do the same with your CV. The grocer might hope that everyone will buy his oranges but he is not surprised or disappointed when people don't. Job seekers should have the same outlook.

On the following letters are extracts, with names which have been disguised, from actual letters leading to an interview which was gained from a cold application. Good covering letters do work!

EXTRACT 1

Polymers Europe Ltd
Sutton
Surrey

2 April 2002

Mr James
5 Navarino Grove
Dalston
E8 1AJ

Dear Mr James

Many thanks for your recent letter and enclosed CV. As I am sure you are well aware, we do not currently have any vacancies at the moment, but nevertheless I have circulated your documents around some of our key managers, and should there be any relevance in talking to you, then you can be assured that we will follow up your approach to us.

Yours sincerely

Miss Cathy Admin

pp James Bigman
Managing Director

EXTRACT 2

Polymers Europe Ltd
Sutton
Surrey

10 April 2002

Mr James
5 Navarino Grove
Dalston
E8 1AJ

Dear Mr James

Further to my letter dated 2nd April 2002, the comments of my colleagues are that we do not have any suitable opportunities for you at BBB. However, we are quite impressed by your skills profile and it occurs to us that this may be of interest to one of our associated companies Polymer Chemicals at Southampton. I have, therefore, passed your papers on to them.

Yours sincerely

James Bigman
Managing Director

CHAPTER 47

A Headhunter Speaks

What follows is a letter from John Courtis of John Courtis & Partners Search and Selection. The letter was sent in response to a cold call to his firm. What John Courtis says makes such sense that the letter, with his permission, appears in full.

Dear

Thank you for your letter and CV. None of our current assignments matches your background and experience. Nonetheless we'll keep your CV on file with pleasure.

However, I am not sure that we are likely to be much use to you. What you have gained is entry to a sort of lottery. The reality of our existence is that we react to what our clients ask us to do. We can't predict what that is likely to be, even for a record like yours.

If you consider the criteria attached to any search or selection assignment you'll recognise that there are almost endless permutations of industry, sector, qualification, age, experience, location and so on. Actually, we receive over ten thousand applications per year but only handle a few hundred jobs.

Add to this the fact that our client list is finite and we are one of many consultancies providing recruitment services, so the odds against a perfect match with you are long. We'd love to help; if only because, when you've got a new job, we hope you may become our client.

My colleague, John McManus, tends to offer ancient wisdom on these occasions. Tell them to write to people who've got jobs to offer, he cries – they're called employers. He doesn't put it prettily, but he's right. Targeting Chief Executives within your area of competence is likely to be more productive. After all, if a job doesn't exist and they like what you say, they can invent one. We cannot.

Yours sincerely,

John Courtis, FCA, MPIM

P.S. Despite what some advisers say, we would appreciate an indication of your last salary. There are both practical and statutory reasons for this. You can tell us what lesser sum you'd accept too, if it's appropriate.

THE EXAMPLES

CVs

CHAPTER 48

The Structure of the CV

There are some traditions and expectations about the structure of CVs, but it is more important that you develop a structure which shows off you and your talents to their best advantage.

The traditional structure, popularly known as 'tombstone', is as follows:

Name
Address
Telephone number
Date of Birth
Marital status and children
Interests/Health
Secondary education
Tertiary education
Professional qualifications
Employment history
(in chronological order)

Our Consultancy has not found this structure as successful as:

Name
Address
Telephone Number
Career Statement or Skills Profile
Career and Achievements to date
(in reverse chronological order)
Professional qualifications and training
Tertiary education
Secondary education
Interests
Personal details

We think this structure achieves more interviews because it delivers information to the potential employer in the order that it is required to make the decision whether or not to interview.

QUALIFICATIONS

Employers are going to be more interested in what you can do in terms of skill and experience before you tell them how old you are or indeed what your interests are. We advocate, for those with recognized and job-relevant qualifications, that these are put after the individual's name on the basis that the employer can see immediately that you are a graduate or that you enjoy an appropriate professional qualification. The education section can then go after your career because the reader already knows what you have achieved in this area.

There is an old adage that it takes 'a good brain to resist an education'. If you have made it to a senior position through a rigorous education in the university of life and hard knocks, then leave the education section out altogether. As we have said elsewhere, employment is about what you can do for an employer and not about how many certificates you can put up on the office wall.

What follows are some examples of various types of CVs. Some much better than others. Please use them as guides where appropriate and do not be tempted to copy. In our experience, applicants who crib chunks from the CVs of others have greater difficulty with their interviews: they have problems substantiating other people's achievements!

EXAMPLE 1: WHAT NOT TO DO

Curriculum Vitae

Name:	David John Applicant
Address:	15 Buckingham Gardens
	Highwood
	London E8 1AJ
Telephone:	020 7923 3456
Date of Birth:	4th April 1951
Place of Birth:	Norbury, South London
Nationality:	British
Marital Status:	Married
Children:	Two aged 10 girl
	14 boy
House:	Owner
Car:	Owner/Driver
Passport:	Holder
Interests:	Music/Photography, Film making,
	Mountaineering, Sound Equipment

QUALIFICATIONS

1968 GCE. O Levels. English Language, English Literature, Mathematics, Science, and Technical Drawing.

1973 Ordinary National Certificate, Electronics and General Engineering (Sutton College).

1974 Apprenticeship with Kent Transformers Ltd with part sandwich degree course at N.E.L. Polytechnic.

1981 Digital Electronics Engineering Course, High Power Ltd, London.

1985 Analogue Data Analysis Short Course, Johnson Ltd, Frimley.

1988 Data Signal Processing Seminar, Monologic Ltd.

1991 Management Training Course, XXX Ltd, (Brighton Polytechnic).

INDUSTRIAL EXPERIENCE
1989 TO 1994

Project Engineer
Optic Power Ltd, Chertsey, Surrey
- Trouble-shooting on site at the Strand Theatre, of Scenery Hoist Control Systems. Including Analogue computing and 415 Volt, 6 Phase Thyrister drive systems.
- Customer presentations and Systems training. Including Digital computing and power drives.
- Specialist power servo products Site Engineer. Including on site problem diagnosis and customer liaison.
- RAF Shoreham, Aircraft wind tunnel development and site engineer. Including Installation Commissioning and testing of computer controlled 415 volt 3 phase drive systems.

1994 to 2000

Principal Systems Engineer/Project Manager
Exim Command and Control Systems Ltd, Croydon, Surrey
- Overall responsibility for up to twelve engineers.
- Management of Control System development (systems, real time software, and servo engineering).
- General Systems Engineering. Including planning of trials and controlling a team to analyze results.
- Systems Engineering enhancement program to introduce improved technique for weapons control, including man-machine interface aspects.
- Development activities on servo systems, involving military vehicle power supplies, trials and analysis.
- Management of software review aspects.
- Chairman of Engineering design reviews.

2000 to 2003

Engineering Manager
Aircraft Systems Ltd, Hawkhurst, Kent

- Group project management of six Sonar Development projects, site and trials work, and studies of various sizes. Total responsibility for thirty engineers, including HR related tasks.
- High level contractual and technical customer liaison and internal liaison including marketing, and business management.
- Quality management.
- Member of factory management team.
- Bid Management, including contract responsibility.

2003 TO PRESENT

Contract Technical Manager
Self-Employed

- Systems Engineering, and consultation of production and product development aspects of photographic studio systems.
- Design of management control and profitability systems.
- Design of financial control and budgeting systems (including management accounting/cash flow control).
- Consultation on production, and pricing strategy.
- Proposal bid and design and development of visual display controller test equipment. Including production and testing.
- Proposal Bids for various design contracts for power supply systems. Including liaison with customers and generation of technical specifications.
- Management of production engineering for the PCB assemblies of a visual display controller system.
- Proposal bid and manufacture of intrared communication system test equipment.

Example 1 – Comments

This is a typical tombstone CV and it can be seen immediately that whilst the information is all there, the potential employer really has to work hard to get at what he or she needs to know to make the important 'must see' decision. Here are just some obvious areas for improvements:

1. There is nothing the employer can buy on the first page. It is all personal details and training, most of which is not relevant to the position being sought.
2. The tombstone layout means that information required by the employer is on the last page.
3. More space is devoted to what was done in the first job 1989 to 1994 than in 2000 to 2003.
4. The job information is all features with little quantification and certainly no benefits.
5. Bald statements such as 'Quality Management' do not mean anything. The employer does not have a crystal ball.
6. Not much thought has been given to the ranking of the responsibilities either in terms of what a potential employer might find exciting or in terms of categories. Engineering and management responsibilities are jumbled up.

EXAMPLE 2

GREG JONES
15 Buckingham Gardens
Dalston
London E8 1AJ
020 7923 3456

PROFILE
A professionally qualified and highly experienced HUMAN RESOURCES SPECIALIST with extensive knowledge and skills in Training and Development, Recruitment and Selection, Career Counselling, Communications and Employee Relations, gained in a wide range of industrial and commercial sectors. Additionally, has organized and lectured on HR and industrial management courses, specializing in organizational behaviour.

KEY SKILLS
- Identifying training and development needs and developing appropriate strategies in support of corporate objectives.
- Designing, developing and implementing training modules and interactive video programs, with an increasing emphasis on management and sales training, and undertaking post-course validation.
- Managing substantial human and financial resources, including a department of 25 staff and an annual budget of £1.8 million.
- Initiating and producing a wide range of training modules, and presenting to all levels of management, up to and including board level.
- Determining and developing management development and succession planning, through management audit, performance reviews and career counselling.

- Selecting and recruiting managerial staff across all functions and disciplines, using psychometric testing and Assessment Centre methodology.
- Lecturing to Polytechnic students and external managers on a wide range of HR and related business subjects.

PROFESSIONAL QUALIFICATIONS
FELLOW OF CHARTERED INSTITUTE OF PERSONNEL AND DEVELOPMENT
MEMBER OF THE INSTITUTE OF TRAINING AND DEVELOPMENT (MITD)

CAREER REVIEW – HIGHLIGHTS
DALSTON BUILDING SOCIETY **1995–Present**

TRAINING MANAGER (REGIONS) 1999–Present
- Created new functions to provide dedicated service to branch network sales force in 375 outlets.
- Recruited and developed training specialists for 12 Regional offices.
- Designed and introduced a portfolio of business development courses, including customer care, sales and territory planning, cross selling, lead general and sales presentation skills.
- Developed customized training modules to meet specific local needs.
- Managed team of 25 specialist and support staff.

TRAINING AND DEVELOPMENT
MANAGER   1998–1999
- Created and introduced an appraisal system for all levels of staff, linked to a performance related pay system, and fostering an achievement oriented culture

- Designed and implemented training courses for assessors, specifically supervisors and above.
- Initiated interactive video as major training medium and produced IV programs on a variety of subjects, including a BIVA award-winning program on 'Assertiveness'.
- Managed team of 25 training professionals, with a budget in excess of £1 million.

MANAGEMENT TRAINING
MANAGER   1997–1998

- Established training as key strategic activity and as a vehicle for cultural and organizational change.
- Developed a new approach to management training, employed TA and other techniques, using cost effective overseas venues.
- Delivered a series of one-week intensive programs to all management staff, including senior managers and directors.
- Marketed and sold courses externally to offset internal costs.

HR MANAGER   1995–1997

- Managed and developed a team of 9 HR professionals and over 62 support staff to cover all HR activities.
- Recruited and selected specialist management staff, for all functional areas.
- Handled and resolved all disciplinary matters referred upwards, sanctioning dismissal where appropriate and managing appeals procedure.
- Undertook salary surveys, recommended level of annual award and negotiated with Staff Association on Conditions of Service and Benefits.

DALSTON AND LINDFIELD
CAREERS SERVICES   1989–1995

DIVISIONAL CAREERS OFFICER
- Managed and developed 11 professional staff in three office locations.
- Determined and implemented annual career counselling and job placement strategy.
- Liaised with careers teachers and lecturers and provided in-service training.
- Provided careers counselling and advice to students and their parents.

Previous HR experience gained in a variety of roles from 1976–83, with HILL SAMUEL, IPC BUSINESS PRESS, NESTLE and MEDICAL RESEARCH COUNCIL. This included employee relations, recruitment and selection and specific project work.

EDUCATION AND TRAINING

LONDON SCHOOL OF ECONOMICS
Postgraduate Diploma in Personnel
Management   1986–1987

SUSSEX COLLEGE FOR THE CAREERS SERVICE
Diploma in Careers Guidance
and Counselling   1988–1989

PERSONAL
Date of Birth: 23 November 1961
Married.

INTERESTS
Amateur Dramatics; Cricket; Rugby; Archery; Anglo-Saxon History; Film Production

Example 2 – Comments
What makes this CV interesting is the Skills summary at the beginning. What is not immediately apparent is that he is not a graduate, although you would expect the sorts of jobs he has done would have such a requirement. This CV shows what can be done to display your skills in the most acceptable way to a prospective employer.

EXAMPLE 3

RICHARD JOHNSON
B.Sc. (Hons), Dip W., MIXX, MIYY

21 Westfield Gardens
Anytown
Herts
AT22 7ZX

0123 123456

Career Summary

A senior marketing professional with significant management experience gained with major US and European high technology multinationals.

An effective thinker and doer offering proven strategic planning, business management and communication skills. Able to work effectively at all levels in organizations with the ability to manage change and achieve commercial profit targets.

Career and Achievements to date:

MARKETING MANAGER,   Jan 01 – present
CUSTOMER SERVICE
FASTGROWTH INC, Smalltown

Responsible for marketing hardware and software services portfolio across ten European countries (>£100M revenue). Managed business development, pricing, competitive analysis and new service development to optimize revenue and customer satisfaction. Developed hardware and software business/pricing models matching revenue to channel and distribution costs. Drove specific marketing programs across Europe. Managed 'end of life' process. A significant part of this role involves the management and successful implementation of change.

SENIOR MARKETING   Sep 99 – Jan 01
CONSULTANT
EUROPEAN WHIZZO LTD, Another city

Managed product life cycle and marketing of UNIX/ Open Systems and networking in the UK's part of XXX's overall computing strategy. Drove two major product line launches in January and May 90. Was instrumental in increasing market share to 8%. Role involved: pricing; product positioning; formulating competitive strategy for UK marketplace. Produced promotional literature. Presented to major retail and government customers and professional bodies. Ran series of sales training courses on the Open Systems and marketplace for > 100 sales people to prepare them to sell these systems to *The Times* 1000 companies. Marketing responsibility for direct and government sales channels. Drove 'Open Systems' message and management interface with X/Open and the DTI.

PRODUCT MARKETING   Mar 98 – Sept 99
MANAGER
LARGE MULTINATIONAL LTD, Greenville

Responsible for development and implementation of marketing strategies for graphics products in UK and Eire and was the primary communications channel between the UK and USA. Conceived and developed new market segments for graphic product – office automaton and process control. Managed OEM and VAR channels for these segments.

SYSTEMS SUPPORT   May 95 – Mar 98
MANAGER
LARGE MULTINATIONAL LTD, Greenville

Built and managed support business with full P&L responsibility, providing pre- and post-sales support for computer aided design tools for the largest customer base outside the USA. Business was consistently managed within budget meeting both revenue and cost objectives. 1987 revenues – £500K. Success came through effective presentation to senior US management, customers, business partners. Negotiated a £350K system hardware and software upgrade contract. Defined contract terms and conditions and produced sales support material. Successfully set up the UK care users' group. Promoted to Product Marketing Manager.

TECHNICAL SUPPORT   Oct 94 – May 95
MANAGER
LARGE MULTINATIONAL LTD, Greenville

Turned round a troubled sales organization in 8 months by setting up a formal software support operation for microprocessor development products running on UNIX and VMS hosts. Raised customer satisfaction levels sufficiently to increase and retain repeat sales business from the installed base. Promoted to Systems Support Manager.

SENIOR ENGINEER   Oct 91 – Oct 94
COMPUTER COMPANY, London

Supported PDP11 and VAX range of processors and

VMS, RSX11 and RSTS/E operating systems. Performed a consultancy role within the support group. Deputized for the group manager to run the day-to-day operations. Additional responsibility for the sale of processor and disk upgrades to the installed base (value £100K) led to an offer of a position as sales executive with target of £1.6M.

ENGINEER   May 90 – Oct 91
COMPUTER COMPANY, London

Account responsible for 20 major sites. Achieved consistently high levels of customer satisfaction as measured by customer surveys. Promoted to Senior Engineer.

SYSTEMS ENGINEER   Jul 88 – May 90
PROCESS INDUSTRY LTD, Oiltown

Position encompassed all aspects of pre-sales support, customer presentations, project management, in-house acceptance and on-site commissioning of high value process control systems in the Oil, Chemical, Pharmaceutical, Power and Water industries, worldwide. Member of the launch team for XXXX systems. Commissioned the first customer systems.

DESIGN ENGINEER   Jul 86 – Jul 88
PROCESS INDUSTRY LTD, Oiltown

Designed analog and digital electronics, microprocessors/miscrosequenced control systems, telemetry systems and interfaces to PDP11 and PDP8 processors. Promoted to Systems Engineer.

Professional and Personal information

Professional: Diploma in something professional
Education establishment 1999
Member of Professional Institution XX
Member of Professional Institution YY

Won the xxxxxxxxxx Award for 2000

Qualifications: BSc. (Hons), 2.1 Electronic Engineering
Good University 1986
GCE A Levels –
  4 Subjects London Board 1983
GCE O Levels –
  11 subjects London Board 1981

Training: Progressive management training
including:
Marketing, Product Marketing,
Direct Marketing, Professional
Selling Skills, Presentation Skills,
Finance, Time Management, Project
Management, Problem Solving
(Advantage & Analytical Trouble
Shooting), Team Building
Various technical training courses
covering hardware, software and
networking

**Outside
Interests:** Elected Chairman of xxxxxxxxxx
Club 1999–2001
Elected Secretary of xxxxxxxxx Club
1998–99
Photography, Bridge, Skiing

Personal: Status: Married, one child
                      Driving Licence: Full UK

Example 3 – Comments
Despite using prose, rather than bullet points, this CV works well. Some of the better points worth mentioning include:

1. The first page includes the career summary. Personally I am not too taken with front pages because it takes the CV into at least three pages. However here the candidate has included his career summary so that there is something the employer can buy on the first page.
2. Job Title is given before the employer and before the dates of the jobs held. Just as well really, because this applicant does not stay in jobs for long. By putting dates on the right hand the jobs tenure, or the lack of it, is not so obvious.
3. Job achievements decrease as we are taken back through the employment history, thus reducing unnecessary information yet having the effects of highlighting current skills and achievements.

EXAMPLE 4

Dominic David Jobs

Résumé

5 Navarino Grove
Dalston
London E8 1AJ
Tel: 020 7932 3456

Has strong technical background including Unix, C, Networks and Graphics and good communication and presentation skills, and a deep understanding of the Unix industry, products and markets. Looking for a role that includes significant customer contact, with the opportunity to contribute to produce and corporate strategy.

Career to date

European Graphics Marketing Manager,
Fastgrowth Europe Inc.   3 yrs

Representing Europe's requirements in Corporate, and providing leadership to the country marketing and sales organizations. Activities include customer presentations, major account support, press interviews, non-disclosure presentations etc. Projects include product introductions and transitions, a server market study (with KPMG) and collateral production, and magazine articles. Contributions made in product positioning and corporate strategy presentations. Covered most product areas in addition to graphics.

Pre-Sales Technical Consultant,
Fastgrowth UK Ltd   4.5 yrs

I was the eleventh employee at Fastgrowth UK, the third software person. Initially covered pre- and post-technical support, specializing in Windows, Graphics and Networking. Presented to customers on many technical and strategic areas and gave some of the early customer and internal training classes. Became the presenter of choice in many subject areas. Installed most of Fastgrowth UK's internal UNIX systems in the early days. Built the European portion of Fastgrowth's XXX/IP wide area network.

Development Engineer, Help Ltd
(Medical Electronics)   6.5 yrs

System, electronics and software design. Later consulting on all development projects. Designed (still) the best selling EMG (neurological diagnostics equipment). Short stay in marketing to launch the product. Introduced C and Unix as the development environment.

Development Engineer, Kind Devices
(Industrial Electronics)   2 yrs

Electronics and software design. Also sys admin & RPG programming of IBM S/32.

Production Test Engineer, Transecon
(Test and Management)   1 yr

Fault finding and calibration of product units.

Lab Technician, New Band
(Bare PCB manufacture)   9 months

Maintenance of etch and plating chemical processes.

Example 4 – Comments
This is an example of an American style CV. Because of the rigorous equality legislation it is not necessary to include much personal information, but this only emphasizes the strength of experience this exceptional candidate offers.

What is good here includes:

1. All the information fits on one page of A4.
2. This candidate in fact has no formal qualification in engineering or computing but has obviously held jobs requiring graduate if not post-graduate status. The education section is omitted but the experience speaks for itself.

CHAPTER 49

Example Career Statements

How these are constructed is outlined Chapter 21. Some Careers Advisers and many head hunters, it should be noted, do not approve of Career Statements because they are subjective and represent the applicant's view of themselves. In my experience employers find them useful. This is ambiguous and confusing but, as was stated in the beginning of the book, there are no absolute rules. You, the reader, will have to decide.

SECRETARIAL AND ADMINISTRATIVE

Experienced executive secretary. Able to work independently and make decisions. Proven administration and organization ability, supported by good interpersonal skills. Used to working with executive management at the highest level.

A technically aware sales co-ordinator who has good communication and organizational skills, able to work at all levels, is committed and can work on her own initiative.

Enthusiastic Customer Service Co-ordinator with proven ability to control multiple marketing projects within given timescales whilst maintaining a high quality of work and achievement of set goals. A confident communicator both internally and externally.

A reliable, conscientious and loyal administrator with good secretarial, accounting and purchasing skills. A skilled negotiator of office equipment and supplies.

MIDDLE AND SENIOR MANAGEMENT

An experienced bi-lingual (English-German) Industrial Designer with an extensive knowledge of the European xxx industry. Particularly strong aesthetic skills combine with a developed understanding of manufacturing requirements and commercial reality.

A qualified and motivated Health Manager who is an innovator with a proven record of achievement in implementing change successfully, founded on a comprehensive experience within the health sector from nursing to management strategy.

A highly experienced, motivated Management Accountant with comprehensive career within the Retail and Leisure industry, wishing to pursue his career in an environment where his financial and inter-personal skills will make a positive contribution.

A professional geologist with excellent experience in exploration, basin synthesis, together with sub-surface operations supported by a good knowledge of contractor services and offering proven skills in database design and management.

Human resource manager with recently developed business analysis – information systems – ability, seeks a human resource management role with an opportunity to develop general management and information management interests in a healthcare context.

EXECUTIVE AND DIRECTORS

A self-motivated and achievement orientated Financial Controller/Director with strong business development skills and a proven record of profit improvement through planning and implementing financial and MIS strategies.

An experienced international general manager with an outstanding track record of maximizing start-up opportunities in highly competitive high technology markets through her high energy, creativity, and a capacity for making things happen.

A confident and creative manager with a proven record of achievement in general and technical management with multinational companies.

A natural team leader in a changing environment with a relaxed style to achieving set goals through the development and motivation of people.

A successful General Manager with Sales and Marketing experience, she utilizes a modern, energetic, versatile and customer oriented style. She advocates teamwork, quality and delegation to build winning profitable companies.

About Transcareer

As you can tell from reading this little book essentially we are psychologists who specialize in all things to do with helping people to be successful in their careers – guidance, advice, coaching, mentoring, assisting individuals with their CVs and even grooming them for interviews.

We work with organizations providing consultancy on devising career development systems and on the people side of mergers, acquisitions and downsizing particularly in the area of outplacement. We also work with individuals from chair person to tea person helping them to become the very best they can.

It does not matter if you represent a large organization or a single individual working on your own, if you would like assistance from the Transcareer team or one of their associates then here are some contact numbers:

In the UK:

In Newcastle	Pat Benson	+44 191 388 9040
In London	Sue Williams	+44 208 987 9725
In Gatwick	Dave Parish	+44 134 271 2345

In Australia:

| In Sydney | Max Eggert | +61 2 9821 1105 |
| In Brisbane | Brian Trevor-Roberts | +61 7 321 77288 |

Or you can contact us on futures@transcareer.com.au

Feedback is useful but please do not send us your CV for comment. We can help you with your CV but we do this for a fee.

We look forward to the opportunity of working with you because your success will be our success.

Perfect Answers to Interview Questions

Max Eggert

All you need to get it right first time

Are determined to succeed in your job search?
Do you want to make sure you stand out from the competition?
Do you want to find out what interviewers *really* want to hear?

Perfect Answers to Interview Questions is essential reading for anyone who's applying for jobs. Written by a leading HR professional with years of experience in the field, it explains the sorts of questions most frequently asked, gives practical advice about how to show yourself in your best light, and provides real-life examples to help you practise at home. Whether you're a graduate looking to take the first step on the career ladder, or you're planning an all-important job change, *Perfect Answers to Interview Questions* will give you the edge.

The *Perfect* series is a range of practical guides that give clear and straightforward advice on everything from getting your first job to choosing your baby's name. Written by experienced authors offering tried-and-tested tips, each book contains all you need to get it right first time.

BOOKS

Perfect Babies' Names

Rosalind Fergusson

All you need to choose the ideal name

Do you want help finding the perfect name?
Are you unsure whether to go for something traditional or something more unusual?
Do you want to know a bit more about the names you are considering?

Perfect Babies' Names is an essential resource for all parents-to-be. Taking a close look at over 3,000 names, it not only tells you each name's meaning and history, it also tells you which famous people have shared it over the years and how popular – or unpopular - it is now. With tips on how to make a shortlist and advice for avoiding unfortunate nicknames, *Perfect Babies' Names* is the ultimate one-stop guide.

BOOKS

Perfect Best Man

George Davidson

All you need to know

Do you want to make sure you're a great best man?
Do you want to make the groom glad he chose you?
Do you need some guidance on your role and responsibilities?

Perfect Best Man is an indispensable guide to every aspect of the best man's role. Covering everything from organising the stag night to making sure the big day runs according to plan, it walks you through exactly what you need to do and gives great advice about getting everything done with the least possible fuss. With checklists to make sure you have it all covered, troubleshooting sections for when things go wrong, and a unique chapter on choosing and organising the ushers, *Perfect Best Man* has everything you need to make sure you rise to the occasion.

BOOKS

Perfect Interview

Max Eggert

All you need to get it right first time

Are you determined to succeed in your job search?
Do you want to make sure you have the edge on the other candidates?
Do you want to find out what interviewers are *really* looking for?

Perfect Interview is an invaluable guide for anyone who's applying for jobs. Written by a leading HR professional with years of experience in the field, it explains how interviews are constructed, gives practical advice about how to show yourself in your best light, and provides real-life examples to help you practise at home. Whether you're a graduate looking to take the first step on the career ladder, or you're planning an all-important job change, *Perfect Interview* will help you stand out from the competition.

BOOKS

ALSO AVAILABLE IN RANDOM HOUSE BOOKS

Perfect Numerical Test Results

Joanna Moutafi and Ian Newcombe

All you need to get it right first time

Have you been asked to sit a numerical reasoning test?
Do you want guidance on the sorts of questions you'll be asked?
Do you want to make sure you perform to the best of your abilities?

Perfect Numerical Test Results is the ideal guide for anyone who
wants to secure their ideal job. Written by a team from Kenexa, one
of the UK's leading compilers of psychometric tests, it explains
how numerical tests work, gives helpful pointers on how to get
ready, and provides professionally constructed sample questions
for you to try out at home. It also contains an in-depth section on
online testing – the route that more and more recruiters are
choosing to take. Whether you're a graduate looking to take the
first step on the career ladder, or you're planning an all-important
job change, *Perfect Numerical Test Results* has everything you
need to make sure you stand out from the competition.

BOOKS

Perfect Personality Profiles

Helen Baron

All you need to get it right first time

Have you been asked to complete a personality questionnaire?
Do you need guidance on the sorts of questions you'll be asked?
Do you want to make sure you show yourself in your best light?

Perfect Personality Profiles is essential reading for anyone who needs to find out more about psychometric profiling. Including everything from helpful pointers on how to get ready to professionally constructed sample questions for you to try out at home, it walks you through every aspect of preparing for a test. Whether you're a graduate looking to take the first step on the career ladder, or you're planning an all-important job change, *Perfect Personality Profiles* has everything you need to make sure you stand out from the competition.

BOOKS

Perfect Psychometric Test Results

Joanna Moutafi and Ian Newcombe

All you need to get it right first time

Have you been asked to sit a psychometric test?
Do you want guidance on the sorts of questions you'll be asked?
Do you want to make sure you perform to the best of your abilities?

Perfect Psychometric Test Results is an essential guide for anyone who wants to secure their ideal job. Written by a team from Kenexa, one of the UK's leading compilers of psychometric tests, it explains how each test works, gives helpful pointers on how to get ready, and provides professionally constructed sample questions for you to try out at home. It also contains an in-depth section on online testing – the route that more and more recruiters are choosing to take. Whether you're a graduate looking to take the first step on the career ladder, or you're planning an all-important job change, *Perfect Psychometric Test Results* has everything you need to make sure you stand out from the competition.

BOOKS

Perfect Pub Quiz

David Pickering

All you need to stage a great quiz

Who invented the cat-flap?
Which is the largest island in the world?
What is tofu made of?

Perfect Pub Quiz is the ideal companion for all general knowledge nuts. Whether you're organising a quiz night in your local or you simply want to get in a bit of practice on tricky subjects, *Perfect Pub Quiz* has all the questions and answers. With topics ranging from the Roman Empire to *Little Britain* and from the Ryder Cup to Alex Rider, this easy-to-use quiz book will tax your brain and provide hours of fun.

BOOKS

Perfect Punctuation

Stephen Curtis

All you need to get it right first time

Do you find punctuation a bit confusing?
Are you worried that your written English might show you up?
Do you want a simple way to brush up your skills?

Perfect Punctuation is an invaluable guide to mastering punctuation marks and improving your writing. Covering everything from semi-colons to inverted commas, it gives step-by-step guidance on how to use each mark and how to avoid common mistakes. With helpful examples of correct and incorrect usage and exercises that enable you to practise what you've learned, *Perfect Punctuation* has everything you need to ensure that you never make a mistake again.

BOOKS

Perfect Readings for Weddings

Jonathan Law

All you need to make your special day perfect

Do you want your wedding to be that little bit more special?
Do you want to personalise the ceremony by including readings that are just right for you?
Do you need help tracking down a traditional reading, or finding something more out of the way?

Perfect Readings for Weddings is an anthology of the best poems, prose passages and quotations about love and marriage. Including everything from familiar blessings and verses to more unusual choices, it covers every sort of reading you could wish for. With advice on how to choose readings that complement one another and tips on how to ensure that everything runs smoothly on the day, *Perfect Readings for Weddings* has everything you need to make sure the whole ceremony is both memorable and meaningful.

BOOKS

Perfect Wedding Speeches and Toasts

George Davidson

All you need to give a brilliant speech

Have you been asked to 'say a few words' on the big day and don't quite know how to go about it?
Do you want easy-to-follow tips on making a speech that is both meaningful and memorable?
Do you want some guidance on how to improve your skills as a public speaker?

Perfect Wedding Speeches and Toasts is an invaluable guide to preparing and delivering unforgettable speeches. Covering everything from advice on mastering your nerves to tips about how to make a real impact, it walks you through every aspect of preparing for the big day and speaking in public. Whether you're the father of the bride, the bride herself, or the best man, *Perfect Wedding Speeches and Toasts* will help make sure your speech goes off without a hitch.

BOOKS

Order more titles in the *Perfect* series
from your local bookshop, or have them delivered
direct to your door by Bookpost.

Perfect Answers to Interview Questions	Max Eggert	9781905211722	£7.99
Perfect Babies' Names	Rosalind Fergusson	9781905211661	£5.99
Perfect Best Man	George Davidson	9781905211784	£5.99
Perfect Interview	Max Eggert	9781905211746	£7.99
Perfect Numerical Test Results	Joanna Moutafi and Ian Newcombe	9781905211333	£7.99
Perfect Personality Profiles	Helen Baron	9781905211821	£7.99
Perfect Psychometric Test Results	Joanna Moutafi and Ian Newcombe	9781905211678	£7.99
Perfect Pub Quiz	David Pickering	9781905211692	£6.99
Perfect Punctuation	Stephen Curtis	9781905211685	£5.99
Perfect Readings for Weddings	Jonathan Law	9781905211098	£6.99
Perfect Wedding Speeches and Toasts	George Davidson	9781905211777	£5.99

Free post and packing
Overseas customers allow £2 per paperback

Phone: 01624 677237

Post: Random House Books
c/o Bookpost, PO Bow 29, Douglas, Isle of Man IM99 1BQ

Fax: 01624 670 923

email: bookshop@enterprise.net

Cheques (payable to Bookpost) and credit cards accepted

Prices and availability subject to change without notice.
Allow 28 days for delivery.
When placing your order, please state if you do not wish to receive any
additional information.

www.randomhouse.co.uk